Moreton Mor

F

sportdesign

four elements

teNeues

sportdesign

four elements

teNeues

Editor:	Paco Asensio
Texts:	Simone K. Schleifer
Research:	Marta Casado
Art Director:	Mireia Casanovas Soley
Layout:	Emma Termes Parera
Spanish translation:	Robert J. Nusbaum
French translation:	Marion Westerhoff
English translation:	Almudena Sasiain

Published by teNeues Publishing Group

teNeues Publishing Company
16 West 22nd Street, New York, NY 10010, USA
Tel.: 001-212-627-9090, Fax: 001-212-627-9511

teNeues Book Division
Kaistraße 18
40221 Düsseldorf, Germany
Tel.: 0049-(0)211-994597-0, Fax: 0049-(0)211-994597-40

teNeues Publishing UK Ltd.
P.O. Box 402
West Byfleet
KT14 7ZF, Great Britain
Tel.: 0044-1932-403509, Fax: 0044-1932-403514

www.teneues.com

ISBN: 3-8238-4562-4

Editorial project: © 2004 **LOFT** Publications

Via Laietana, 32 4º Of. 92
08003 Barcelona, Spain
Tel.: 0034 932 688 088
Fax: 0034 932 687 073
e-mail: loft@loftpublications.com
www.loftpublications.com

Printed by: Anman Gràfiques del Vallès, Spain. April 2004

While we strive for utmost precision in every detail, we cannot be held responsible for any inaccuracies, neither for any subsequent loss or damage arsing.

Bibliographic information published by Die Deutsche Bibliothek. Die Deutsche Bibliothek lists this publication in the Deutsche Nationalbibliographie; detailed bibliographic data is available in the Internet at http://dnb.ddb.de.

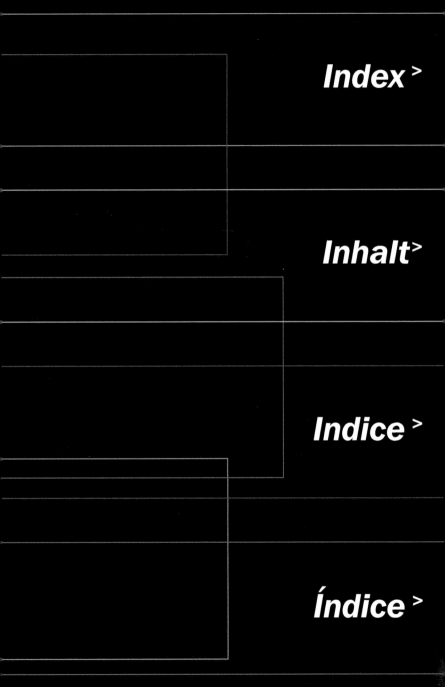

Index >

Inhalt >

Indice >

Índice >

Introduction >

Einleitung >

Introduction >

Introducción >

Sports keep us fit and healthy. It's simply wonderful to leave your everyday cares behind and devote yourself to physical fitness by exercising your body and feeling its energy. There's nothing like sports for creating the perfect equilibrium between body and soul. And today's society gives us countless opportunities to become active. People of all ages can readily find the kind of sports activity that's right for them, whether it's bungee jumping or meditative lap swimming.

When we think of our planet in terms of the elements air, earth, water, ice and snow, we realize that modern technology has eliminated the obstacles to delving into these realms. Today we can explore the ocean floor, high mountain peaks and even glide through the air. Wherever our sporting proclivities take us, high tech materials are an indispensable prerequisite for untrammeled enjoyment. And the watchword today is "ultralight", whether for gliding, water skiing, snowboarding or climbing—for which the weight of the materials used is constantly being reduced through technological innovations.

And wherever materials come into play, the question of aesthetics is never far behind. Material designers strive to marry function to form and the practical to the aesthetic. Safety, stability and user friendliness are absolute musts, which is why products such as hybrid bikes, fibreglass-skiboards or air-cushioned shoes, and are solidly constructed to rigorous specifications.

Thus, the aesthetic aspect plays a key role since sports are much more than just a matter of doing exercise. They're a life style unto themselves—a realm of activity that is inextricably bound up with freedom, relaxation and enjoyment. And thus we expect the designs of the sports equipment we use to reflect and be an expression of our personalities.

We invite you to explore the world of sports equipment design on the following pages, which contain a selection of some of today's most innovative and cutting edge products presented under four rubrics: snow, air, earth and water. We hope you will enjoy and be inspired by these striking designs from around the world—designs that are sure to quicken the pulse of athletes and non-athletes alike.

Sport hält uns fit und gesund! Wie herrlich ist es, den Alltag hinter sich zu lassen und sich ganz seinem Körper zu widmen, ihn zu bewegen und seine Energie zu spüren. Durch nichts können wir so einfach die Balance zwischen Leib und Seele herstellen wie durch Sport. Wir haben heutzutage eine unbegrenzte Vielfalt an Möglichkeiten um aktiv zu werden. Ob jung oder alt, ob auf die extreme Art beim Bungeejumping oder eher meditativ beim Yoga – mit Sicherheit kann jeder Mensch für sich persönlich genau das Richtige finden.

Teilen wir unseren Erdball in die Elemente Luft, Erde und Wasser sowie Eis bzw. Schnee ein, so stellen wir fest, dass uns dank modernster Entwicklungen keine Grenzen mehr gesetzt sind: So können wir die Tiefen der Meeresgründe, die Höhen der Gipfel erforschen und sogar durch die Lüfte gleiten. Um den Sport immer und überall in vollen Zügen genießen zu können, sind hochentwickelte Materialien die absolute Voraussetzung. „Ultraleicht" heißt die Devise – egal ob beim Segelfliegen, Wasserski, Snowboarden oder Klettern: Das Gewicht der verwendeten Stoffe wird durch ständige Überarbeitung und Erneuerung immer weiter reduziert.

< 12

13 >

Und überall, wo es um Materialien geht, taucht unwillkürlich auch die Frage nach dem Design auf. Dieses hat die Aufgabe, die Verbindung zwischen Zweckmäßigkeit und Schönheit herzustellen, zwischen praktischen und ästhetischen Gesichtspunkten. Sicherheit, Stabilität und einfache Benutzung müssen gewährleistet sein, und so finden wir vom Urban Hybrid Bike über die luftgepolsterten Schuhe bis hin zum Glasfaser Skiboard stets eine solide und präzise Verarbeitung.

Auch die Ästhetik hat einen hohen Stellenwert, denn Sport ist für uns weitaus mehr als nur die rein körperliche Betätigung. Er ist Lebensstil und steht für Freizeit, Freiheit, Erholung und Spaß. Und ebenso erwarten wir auch ein Design, das unsere Persönlichkeit unterstreicht und widerspiegelt.

Begeben Sie sich auf den folgenden Seiten in die Welt des Sportdesigns. Sie finden eine Auswahl der innovativsten und modernsten Produkte, unterteilt in die vier Kapitel „Schnee", „Luft", „Erde" und „Wasser". Lassen Sie sich verführen und inspirieren von ausgefallenen Designs aus der ganzen Welt, die nicht nur die Herzen der Sportler höher schlagen lassen.

Le sport nous aide à maintenir la forme et la santé! Quel délice de laisser le quotidien derrière soi et de se consacrer entièrement au bien-être de son corps, de bouger et sentir l'énergie en soi. Il n'y a rien de mieux que le sport pour nous permettre de rétablir si facilement l'équilibre entre le corps et l'esprit. Aujourd'hui, nous disposons d'une multitude infinie de possibilités pour devenir actif. Jeune ou âgé, que ce soit en pratiquant un sport extrême comme le saut à l'élastique ou tout simplement la méditation comme le Yoga – il est sûr que chacun de nous y trouve exactement son bonheur personnel.

Si nous prenons notre globe sous l'aspect des éléments, air, terre et eau y compris la glace et la neige, force est de constater que les développements techniques les plus récents reculent les frontières de l'impossible : en effet, nous pouvons explorer les fonds marins, les plus hauts sommets et même planer dans l'air. Pour profiter du sport à fond, à tous moments et en tous lieux, il est absolument indispensable d'avoir du matériel hautement performant. « Ultra léger » telle est la devise – que ce soit pour le vol à voile, le ski nautique, le surf des neiges ou l'escalade, le poids des matières utilisées ne cesse d'être réduit grâce à des modifications et des nouveautés constantes.

‹ 14

15 ›

Et partout, matériel et design vont instinctivement de pair. Le design est là pour joindre l'utile à l'agréable, pour unir idées pratiques et esthétiques. Il faut garantir la sécurité, la stabilité et la simple utilisation, conditions que nous retrouvons dans l'éventail de produits allant de Durban Hybride Pike en passant par les chaussures à coussin d'air jusqu'aux skiboards en fibre de verre.

L'esthétique est très importante car le sport est pour nous bien plus qu'une simple activité physique. C'est un style de vie et il est synonyme de loisir, liberté, détente et plaisir. C'est pourquoi nous attendons du design qu'il reflète et mette en valeur notre personnalité.

Les pages suivantes, vous feront entrer dans le monde du design adapté au sport. Vous y trouverez une sélection de produits les plus innovants et les plus modernes répartis en quatre chapitres « Neige », « Air », « Terre » et « Eau ». Laissez vous séduire et inspirer par les designs remarquables du monde entier. Sportif ou non, vous serez enthousiasmés au plus haut point.

El deporte nos mantiene sanos y en forma. Qué agradable es, tras finalizar la jornada diaria, dedicarse por completo a cuidar el cuerpo, a moverlo, a sentir su energía. Y es que nada mejor que el deporte para lograr el equilibrio entre cuerpo y alma. En la actualidad, hay un sinfín de posibilidades de permanecer activo, tanto para jóvenes como para no tan jóvenes, con deportes extremos como el puenting o más bien meditativos como el yoga; todos con seguridad pueden encontrar la práctica que más se adapte a sus gustos y necesidades.

Si dividimos el globo terrestre en los elementos aire, tierra, agua y nieve o hielo, nos daremos cuenta de que gracias a los modernos avances tecnológicos han desaparecido muchas de las tradicionales limitaciones. De este modo es posible explorar el fondo de profundos mares, ascender a la cima de las montañas más altas e, incluso, planear en el aire. Pero para disfrutar plenamente del deporte en cualquier lugar es absolutamente imprescindible utilizar materiales de óptima calidad: el término ultraligero es el lema, ya se trate de vuelo a vela, esquí acuático, snowboard o escalada.

< 16
17 >

Y por supuesto, siempre que se habla de materiales surge la cuestión del diseño. Este tiene el objetivo de armonizar la funcionalidad y la belleza, los planteamientos prácticos y estéticos. La seguridad, la estabilidad y la manejabilidad son imprescindibles y, por ello, tanto la bicicleta híbrida urbana como zapatillas con cámara de aire o una tabla de skiboard de fibra óptica mostrarán siempre una fabricación sólida y precisa.

Pero también la estética tiene un alto valor, ya que consideramos el deporte como algo más que el mero ejercicio del culto al cuerpo. Para nosotros es un estilo de vida y supone tiempo libre, descanso, diversión, libertad. Por tanto, esperamos también un determinado diseño que subraye y refleje nuestra personalidad.

Adéntrese, a través de las siguiente páginas, en el universo del diseño deportivo. Encontrará una amplia selección de los productos más innovadores y modernos divididos en cuatro capítulos: "Nieve", "Aire", "Tierra" y "Agua". Déjese seducir e inspirar por los diseños más destacados de todo el mundo, que no solamente llegan al corazón de los deportistas.

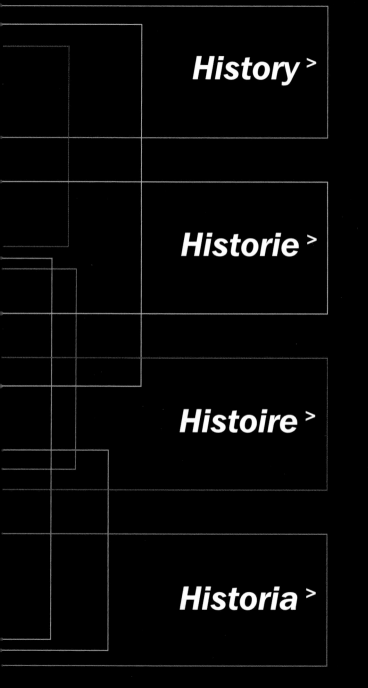

History ˃

Historie ˃

Histoire ˃

Historia ˃

Sports have been a feature of all cultures and civilizations throughout human history. For example, in 776 BC, the Greeks began holding the Olympic games every four years. And in France, archaeologists have uncovered remnants of 20,000 year old bear dummies which are thought to have been used for spear throwing practice. The Chinese are credited with the invention of soccer by virtue of having, as early as the 4th century BC, played a similar game using a leather ball filled with feathers. And skiing is as old as the wheel. Over 4,000 years ago, people living in the mountains of northern Europe used ski-like boards to move around on snow covered surfaces. And back then, as today, inventiveness abounded: willow twigs were used as bindings for these early skis.

Metals and synthetic materials came increasingly into use in the mid-19th century, and this period also saw the first attempts to create aesthetically pleasing designs. In 1870 the Norwegian Sondre A. Norheim invented shaped skis that allowed the skier to turn more easily—but these skis were rather drab in color. During this period the main criteria for sports equipment design was function, as well as the nature of the materials being used. Only in the early 20th century did designers begin to strive for aesthetically pleasing shapes and colors. And from this point on things really took off, leading eventually to what we today call sports product design—the creation of products that constitute a happy marriage between form and function. High tech materials and innovative designs render today's athletic activities highly pleasurable, leading us to wonder what kinds of ingenious creations the future holds in store.

< 20

21 >

Sport hat es zu allen Zeiten und bei allen Völkern gegeben. Schon im antiken Griechenland wurden seit 776 v. Chr. alle vier Jahre die Olympischen Spiele ausgetragen. Noch viel weiter zurück führen Spuren nach Frankreich, wo Wissenschaftler 20.000 Jahre alte Bärenattrappen entdeckten, die vermutlich zum Speerwurftraining dienten. Als Erfinder des Fußballs gelten die Chinesen, die bereits im 4. Jahrhundert vor unserer Zeitrechnung ein ähnliches Spiel ausübten und zu jener Zeit eine mit Federn gefüllte Lederkugel als Ball benutzten. Und der Ski ist sogar älter als das Rad, denn schon vor mehr als 4000 Jahren wurden im hohen Norden Europas Ski-ähnliche Bretter zur Fortbewegung im Schnee benutzt. An Kreativität hat es nie gemangelt, und so flochten die Menschen die ersten Bindungen aus Weidenzweigen.

Materialien wie Metalle und Kunststoffe gewannen Mitte des 19. Jahrhunderts immer mehr an Bedeutung und aus dieser Zeit stammen auch erste Ansätze eines künstlerisch gestalteten Designs. Der Norweger Sondre A. Norheim erfand 1870 den taillierten Ski, der ein besseres Kurvenfahren ermöglicht, jedoch rein optisch noch etwas farblos war. Zu dieser Zeit wurde die Form eines Sportobjektes vorrangig von ihrer Funktion und dem verwendeten Stoff bestimmt und erst seit Anfang des 20. Jahrhunderts begann man, äußere Erscheinung und Ästhetik mit zu berücksichtigen. Von hier an schreitet die Entwicklung rasant voran und führt uns schließlich zu dem, was wir heutzutage unter Sportdesign verstehen – die Schaffung von Produkten, bei denen Schönheit und Funktionalität im Einklang stehen. Modernste High-Tech-Materialien und fantasievolle Entwürfe machen heute den Sport auch zum ästhetischen Hochgenuss und lassen uns gespannt auf die Innovationen der Zukunft hoffen.

Le sport a existé de tout temps et en tous lieux. Dès 776 av.
J. C., la Grèce antique organisait déjà les jeux olympiques tous
les quatre ans. Ses traces remontent encore plus loin dans le
temps, en France, où les scientifiques ont découvert des ours
factices vieux de 20.000 ans qui ont pu servir à l'entraînement
des lanceurs de javelot. On pense que les Chinois ont inventé le
football car déjà au 4éme siècle avant notre ère, ils pratiquaient
un jeu similaire avec, à l'époque, une boule de cuir remplie de
plumes pour ballon. Le ski est même plus ancien que la roue.
En effet, il y a plus 4000 ans, on utilisait déjà dans le grand
Nord de l'Europe des planches en guise de skis pour se dépla-
cer dans la neige. Les hommes qui ne manquaient donc pas
d'imagination, tissèrent les premières fixations en osier.

Au milieu du 19éme siècle, le métal et les matières plastiques
gagnent en importance et c'est aussi à cette époque que l'idée
d'un design artistique fait ses premiers pas. En 1870, le Norvé-
gien Sondre A. Norheim invente le ski cintré plus facile à ma-
nœuvrer dans les virages mais toutefois encore quelconque sur
le plan optique. En ce temps là, la forme d'un article de sport
dépendait avant tout de sa fonction et des matières employées.
Ce n'est qu'au début du 20éme siècle que l'on commence à
tenir compte de l'aspect extérieur et de l'esthétique. Dès lors,
l'évolution se fait à pas de géant pour arriver enfin à notre
notion actuelle du design dans le domaine sportif – la création
de produits en harmonie avec beauté et fonctionnalité. Les
matières les plus modernes à haute performance technique et
les projets plein d'imagination font du sport un plaisir esthétique
et nous laissent dans l'expectative des innovations futures.

El deporte ha existido en todas las épocas y en todas las culturas. Ya en la antigua Grecia, desde el 776 a. C. se celebraban cada cuatro años los Juegos Olímpicos. Y en Francia, algunos arqueólogos han encontrado restos de más de 20.000 años de antigüedad: unas figuras similares a osos artificiales que al parecer servían a los hombres para entrenarse en el arte de cazar con lanzas. Los chinos están considerados como los inventores del fútbol, ya que en el siglo IV de nuestra era practicaban un juego similar con una pelota rellena de plumas. Y el esquí es tan antiguo como la rueda, ya que en el norte de Europa se han encontrado restos de tablas de más de 4.000 años de antigüedad utilizadas para avanzar por la nieve. El ser humano, nunca carente de creatividad, las fijaba a los pies con mimbre.

Materiales como el metal y el plástico adquirieron cada vez más importancia en el siglo XIX y precisamente en esa época se establecieron los cimientos del diseño artístico actual. El noruego Sondre A. Norheim descubrió en 1870 el esquí tallado, que permitía tomar mejor las curvas, pero que desde el punto de vista visual resultaba un poco pobre. Y es que en aquel tiempo, se daba más importancia a la funcionalidad de un objeto deportivo y al material utilizado que a su forma. Sólo a principios del siglo XX se empezó a tener en cuenta la estética. Desde entonces, el desarrollo fue rapidísimo y condujo a lo que en la actualidad entendemos como diseño deportivo, es decir, la creación de productos que armonizan belleza y funcionalidad. Los materiales creados con la más moderna tecnología y los diseños llenos de fantasía hacen hoy en día del deporte una actividad totalmente placentera, también desde el punto de vista estético, y nos permiten esperar futuras innovaciones.

> Alabaster peaks, swooping slopes and glittering ice crystals that refract the sun like a thousand diamonds—surely a sight to set many a pulse racing. And some enthusiasts even enjoy the pleasures of winter year round, immersing themselves in the snowy world whenever the opportunity arises. Winter sports have become ever more colorful in recent years thanks to the multiplicity of apparatuses that whisk us down the slopes—whether it's traditional skis, snowboards, monoskis or carving skis. The sky appears to be the limit in this realm, and every year brings with it new conveyances by descending snow-packed inclines. Ski fashions are exciting and richly colorful as well—a confluence of new fabrics, functions and elegance. And those who do not find vertiginous crystalline slopes to their liking can still enjoy the snow by going cross country skiing, snowshoeing or sledding.

> Weiß getünchte Gipfel, Steilhänge und glitzernde Eiskristalle, in denen sich das Sonnenlicht bricht – dieser Anblick lässt die Herzen vieler Menschen höher schlagen. So manch einer freut sich schon das ganze Jahr auf die Wintersaison, wenn es endlich wieder soweit ist einzutauchen in die weiße Welt. In den letzten Jahren wurden die Wintersportgebiete immer bunter dank der Vielfalt an Sportgeräten, mit denen wir die Abhänge hinuntergleiten, seien es die klassischen Skier, Snowboards, Monoskis oder der Carving Ski. Der Phantasie und dem Erfindungsgeist sind keine Grenzen gesetzt, und jedes Jahr entdecken wir neue Gefährte auf den Pisten. Bunt und einfallsreich ist auch die Mode, in der perfekt neue Materialien, Funktionalität und Eleganz kombiniert werden. Und wem die steilen Hänge nicht so behagen, der hat die Möglichkeit bei Langlauf, Schlittschuhlauf oder beim Rodeln die Winterlandschaft zu genießen.

> Cimes badigeonnées de blanc, descente à pic et cristaux de glace étincelants réfractant la lumière du soleil – nombreux sont ceux dont le cœur bat plus byt devant un tel spectacle. D'aucuns se réjouissent toute l'année en pensant à l'hiver et au moment où ils pourront plonger enfin dans la blancheur du monde enneigé. Au cours de ces dernières années, les domaines de sports d'hiver se sont de plus en plus colorés sous la multitude de matériel sportif mis à notre disposition pour descendre les pistes, que ce soit les skis classiques, les surfs des neiges, les monoskis ou encore les skis carving. Il n'y a plus aucune limite à l'imagination et à l'esprit d'invention. Chaque année nous découvrons du nouveau matériel de glisse sur la piste. La mode, elle aussi, est multicolore et pleine de trouvailles dans l'art de combiner parfaitement nouvelles matières, fonctionnalité et élégance. Ceux qui ne sont pas trop attirés par les descentes à pic, peuvent faire du ski de fond, du patin à glace ou de la luge pour profiter du paysage hivernal.

> Las cimas y las pendientes blancas y los brillantes cristales de hielo en los que rompe la luz del sol constituyen una indescriptible visión que acelera el latido de los corazones de quienes lo contemplan; estas personas esperan todo el año con impaciencia la llegada de la temporada de invierno para sumergirse en este paraíso blanco. En los últimos tiempos, los deportes de invierno han ganado cada vez más adeptos gracias a las diferentes modalidades de descenso en montañas, desde el clásico esquí, hasta otras prácticas como el snowboard, el monoesquí o el esquí carving. La fantasía y el espíritu de innovación ya no tienen límites y año tras año descubrimos nuevos compañeros sobre las pistas. La moda en el esquí es colorida y variada, acorde con la creación de nuevos materiales que combinan funcionalidad y elegancia. Y para todos aquellos a los que no les seduzcan las pendientes, siempre queda la posibilidad de disfrutar de los paisajes nevados mientras practican esquí de fondo, patinaje sobre hielo o carreras en trineo.

Helmet Collection
Automatic *by K2*

< 32

33 >

Mountain
by Völkl

Capsule
by K2

Cyclone Leather
by K2

Cyclone Pipe
by K2

Racer
by Tecnica

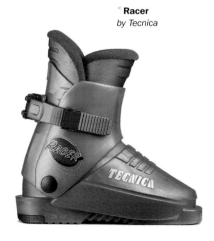

< **Rival X5**
by Tecnica

< **Rival X7**
by Tecnica

< **Rival X9**
by Tecnica

Rival X8
y Tecnica

^{<} **Rival X9**
by Tecnica

^{<} 34

35 ^{>}

^{<} **Icon Race**
by Tecnica

< Theorem
by Burton

< Halcyon
by Burton

< Figmen
by Burton

< Anagram
by Burton

< Theorem Darkslide
by Burton

Poles >
by Burton

< **Probe**
by Burton

Porsche GT S
by Völkl

< **V-Ski**
by Völkl

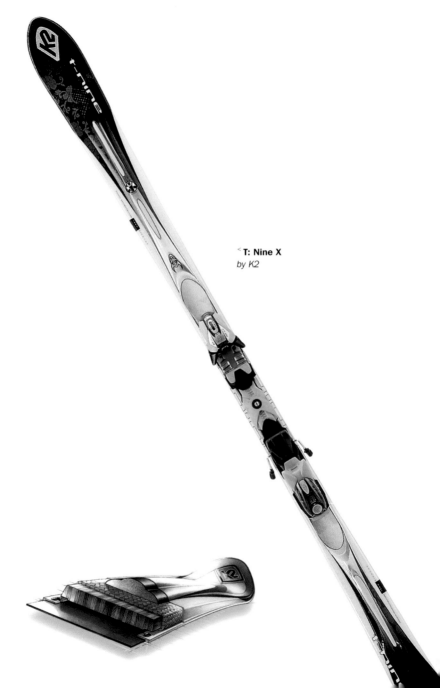

T: Nine X
by K2

< **Shuksan**
by K2

< **8611 AT-Ascent**
by K2

< **Axis AK**
by K2

< **Phat Luv**
by K2

< M 700
by Marker

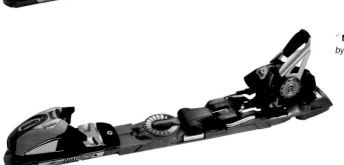

< M 1000
by Marker

< M 1100
by Marker

< Titanium 1200
by Marker

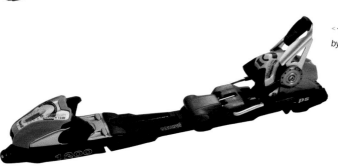

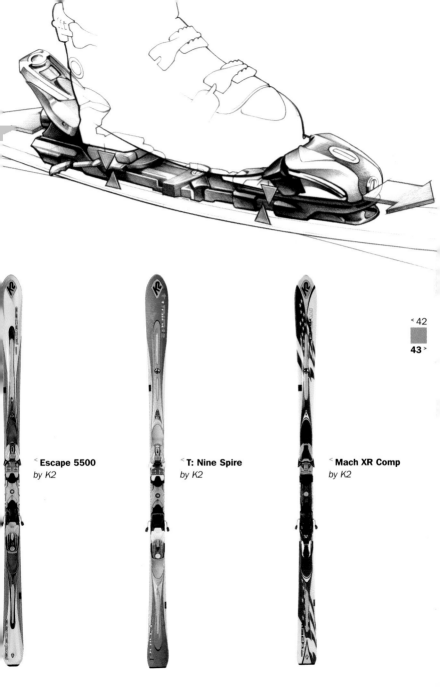

Escape 5500
by K2

T: Nine Spire
by K2

Mach XR Comp
by K2

< 42
43 >

7S Concept
by Tecnica

< 44
45 >

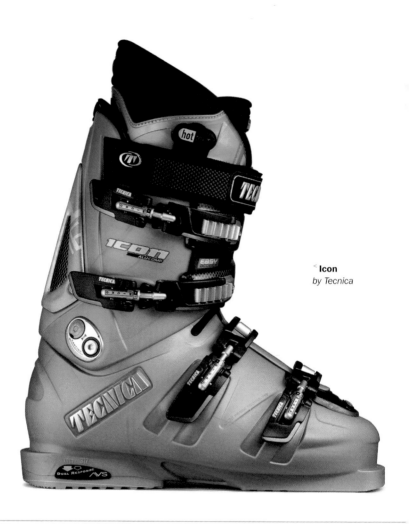

[＜] **Icon**
by Tecnica

[＜] **Icon**
by Tecnica

Icon >
by Tecnica

< 46

47 >

< **Icon**
by Tecnica

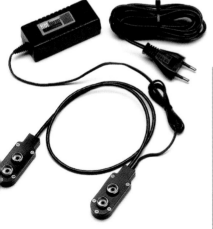

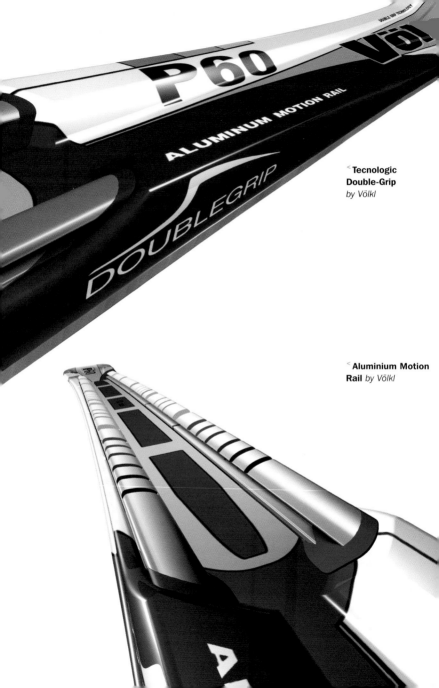

< **Tecnologic Double-Grip** *by Völkl*

< **Aluminium Motion Rail** *by Völkl*

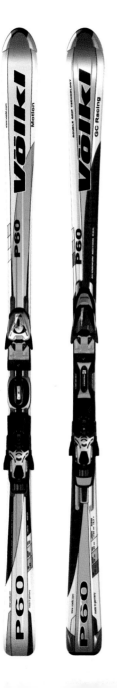

^{<} **Rental Series**
Big Air *by K2*

^{<} **Rental Series**
Fatty *by K2*

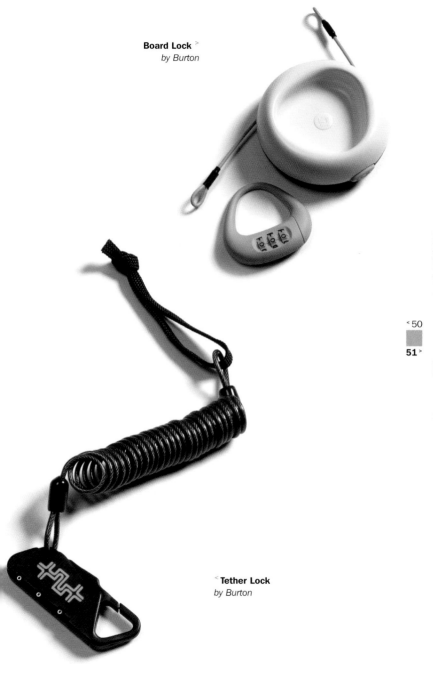

Board Lock >
by Burton

< 50

51 >

< **Tether Lock**
by Burton

4 Speed
by K2

5 Speed
by K2

6 Speed
by K2

Axis XT >
by K2

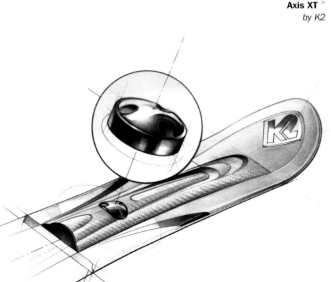

< AK Paradise
by Burton

Infantry Pack
Burton

< Day Hiker
by Burton

< Premium Pack
by Burton

< 55 Pack
by Burton

< 7 Senses.5
by Tecnica

Energy >
by Völkl

[<] **M 450**
by Marker

[<] **Comp 1400**
by Marker

[<] **Mrr 1500**
by Marker

[<] **M 1000 Comp Jr**
by Marker

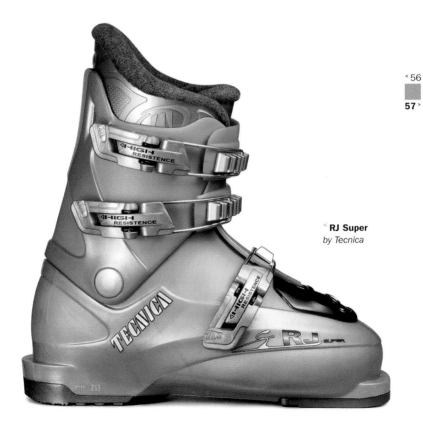

< **RJ Super**
by Tecnica

Supersport >
by Völkl

7-24 >
by Völkl

< **Expression**
by Völkl

Entryx RT
by Tecnica

Entryx RT >
by Tecnica

< **Entryx RT**
by Tecnica

< 58

59 >

Rival RT7
by Tecnica

Rival RT7 >
by Tecnica

< **Rival RX**
by Tecnica

< **Rival RX**
by Tecnica

Rival RX
by Tecnica

< **Rival RX**
by Tecnica

< **Supersport**
by Völkl

Snowboard
< **Custom X**
by Burton

< Halcyon
by Burton

< WMS Toaster
by Burton

Snowboarding Boot
< C 16
by Burton

Circuit Pack
Burton

‹ **Skycap**
by Burton

Snowboarding Boots
‹ **SL 6**
by Burton

[<] **Logo Slider Cap**
by Burton

[<] **Old School B-Ball**
by Burton

[<] **Ronin Weave Cap**
by Burton

[<] **Leather Cap**
by Burton

[<] **AK Continuum
Fuse Mitt**
by Burton

< **Snowdeck Approach**
by Burton

Snowboard
Satellite [>]
by K2

Snowboard
[<] **Satellite Wide**
by K2

Snowboarding Boots

< **Custom**
by Burton

Snowboarding
< T6
by Burton

< **Ruler**
by Burton

< **Lens Tints**
by Burton

Tuning Vises >
by Burton

< **Aluminium Logo Mats**
by Burton

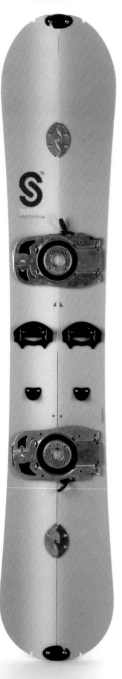

Snowboard

‹ **S-Series**
by Burton

^{<} 74

75 ^{>}

^{<} **PSI**
by Burton

< **Leather
Glove Simply**
by Burton

< **Leather
Glove Taupe**
by Burton

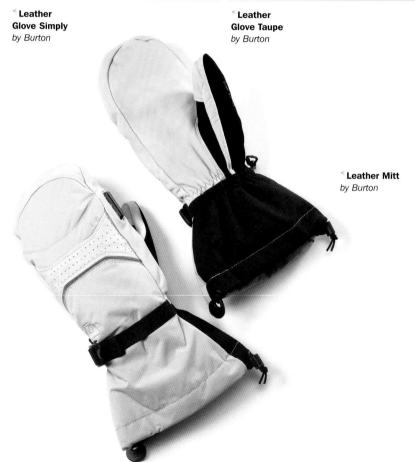

< **Leather Mitt**
by Burton

[<] **P1 MD**
by Burton

Snowboard
[<] **Feather**
by K2

[<] **Syncro**
by Burton

< **Board Sac**
by Burton

< **Board Chamber**
by Burton

< **Wheelie Board Case**
by Burton

< **Wheelie Gig Bag**
by Burton

Space Sack >
by Burton

< **Hemp Cadet**
by Burton

< **Nemesis**
by K2

Halcyon (Gear Box)
by Burton

Squamie >
by Burton

JUNKYARD

‹ **Snowdeck Junkyard**
by Burton

<Board Sleeve
by Burton

SI Midnight >
by Burton

< **Foundation SI**
by Burton

< 82

83 >

Snowboarding Boots
< **WMS Flament SI**
by Burton

Ski and Snowboard Helmet

‹ **Shaun White**
by Red

Remix
by Red

Agent >
by Red

Synth
by Red

< 84

85 >

Hifi >
by Red

Buzzcap
by Red

MT 1 >
by Red

Snowboarding

< **Access**
by K2

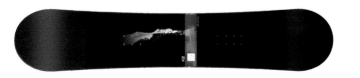

⌃ **Bullet Tool**
by Burton

⌃ **Clicker Plasma**
by K2

⌃ **Clicker Magma**
by K2

Snowboarding Boots

Raider
by K2

< **Luna Women's**
by K2

< **Women's T1**
by K2

< **Boomer Women's**
by K2

< **Freestyle**
by Burton

< **Wheelie Locker**
by Burton

< **Boneout Sock**
by Burton

< **Ultra Wool Sock**
by Burton

< 90
91 >

< **Emblem Sock**
by Burton

Kron Tool >
by Burton

< **Hot Stick-Iron**
by Burton

Zip Tool >
by Burton

< **Cypher**
by Burton

< **WMS Visor**
by Burton

PSI >
by Burton

< **Driver**
by Burton

Foundation >
by Burton

Snowboard

< **Luna**
by K2

< **Nugget Tool**
by Burton

< **Ninjaclava**
by Burton

Impact Wrist Guards >
by Burton

< **Skullcap**
by Burton

Snowboarding

Baron >
by Burton

Snowboarding Boots

< **V12 Magma**
by K2

Driver
Burton

Mission >
by Burton

< **Teaser Pack**
by Burton

< **Moto**
by Burton

Snowboarding
Instinct ^{>}
by K2

^{<} 100

101 ^{>}

^{<} **Support Glove**
by Burton

^{<} **RPM Leather Glove**
by Burton

Snowboard

Code >
by Burton

Pipe Glove >
by Burton

Freestyle V11 >
by Burton

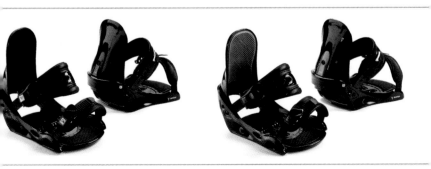

[<] **Chenille Rib Beanie**
by Burton

[<] **Wms Radar Gatsby**
by Burton

[<] **Grom Reversible Beanie** *by Burton*

[<] **Earflap Hat**
by Burton

[<] **Freestyle Jr.**
by Burton

Logo Beanie
by Burton

< **Hood Band**
by Burton

< **Wms Reverse Radar**
by Burton

< **Criss Cross Beanie**
by Burton

< 104

105 >

Snowboard
< **LTR**
by Burton

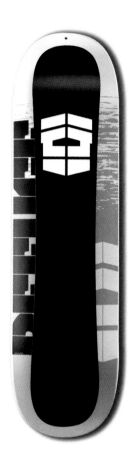

Snowdeck Junkyard
by Burton

AK Down Jacket >
by Burton

< 106
107 >

Shield Pant
by Burton

6/4 Down Jacket
by Burton

Tribute >
by Burton

MS Shield Pant
Burton

<**AK Down Jacket**
by Burton

Sable >
by Burton

Shaun >
by Burton

Stiletto
Burton

< 110

111 >

Lexa
Burton

P1 HD
Burton

[<] **Warrior**
by Forum

[<] **Warrior**
by Forum

[<] **Devun
Walsh**
by Forum

[<] **Dev
Wals**
by Fo

[<] **Division**
by Forum

[<] **Division**
by Forum

[<] **Raider**
by Forum

[<] **Rai**
by Fo

Team
by Forum

Team
by Forum

Star
by Forum

Star
by Forum

Women's Recon
by Forum

Women's Recon
by Forum

Youngblood
by Forum

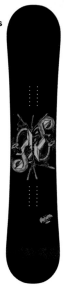

Youngblood
by Forum

The Mocean
by Porsche

 GRD/0001
by CliC Goggles

 GRD/0002
by CliC Goggles

[<] 114

115 [>]

 GRD/0003
by CliC Goggles

[<] **GRD/0010**
by CliC Goggles

[<] **GRD/0012**
by CliC Goggles

^{<}**Suunto Replacing Luck**
by Suunto Wristop Computers

^{<}**Suunto Regatta. Marine. Time,
Sailing Conditions, Computer,
Chronograph**
by Suunto Wristop Computers

Suunto S6. Snow Sports. Time Computer, Chronograph, Weather, Altimeter
Suunto Wristop Computers

Suunto Altimax. Snow Sports. Time, Chronograph, Barometer, Altimeter
by Suunto Wristop Computers

Suunto X6. Cross Sports
by Suunto Wristop Computers

**Suunto Escape 203. Cross Sports.
Altimeter, Barometer, Time**
by Suunto Wristop Computers

Suunto G9. Golf. Course, Game, Weather, Computer, Time
by Suunto Wristop Computers

Argon System Extreme
by Vaude

Altitude Jacket III
by Vaude

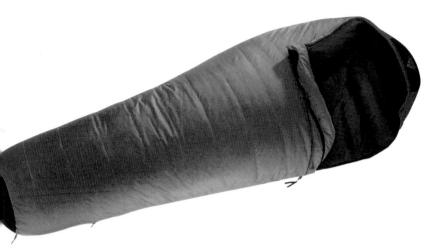

Down 90/10. Polar Light. Sleeping Bag
Vaude

Avalanche Shovel

< **Backcountry Rescue**
by Vaude

< **Backcountry Pro**
by Vaude

< **Lexan**
by Vaude

< **Backcountry Light**
by Vaude

Alpine Harness
< **Edelweiß Rodeo**
by Vaude

Climbing Helmet
< **Lucky Alpha**
by Vaude

< **Diamir Titanal 3**
by Fritschi

< **Diamir Freeride**
by Fritschi

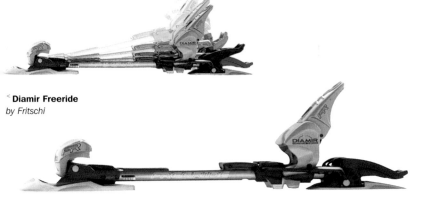

Diamir Freeride
by Fritschi

Snowboard

Premier
by Rossignol

Motion Wide
by Hammer

< **SiiS2**
*by Step In SIS2/
Rossignol*

Snowboarding Boots

< **SiiS2**
by Step In SIS2/Rossignol

< **Série Soft**
by Rossignol

‹ **Bogner Allmountain**
by Bogner

‹ **Bogner Carving**
by Bogner

‹ **Bogner Bigmountain**
by Bogner

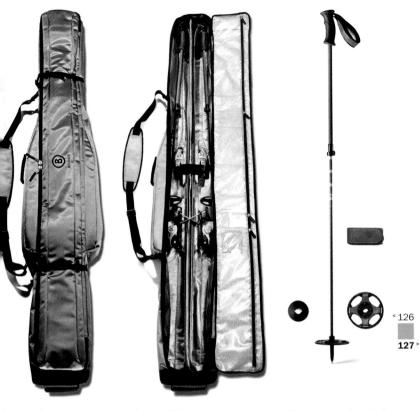

< 126

127 >

< **Bogner Ski Tasche**
by Bogner

< **Bogner Ski Set**
by Bogner

< **Bogner Teleskopstock**
by Bogner

< **Bogner Skischloss**
by Bogner

< **Bogner Customer Card**
by Bogner

[<] **Boys**
by Quiksilver

[<] 128

129 [>]

[<] **Multipurpose**
by Quiksilver

< **Performance**
by Roxy

< 130
131 >

< **X Series**
by Roxy

< Performance
by Roxy

< X Series
by Roxy

> "Free as a bird" is something we tend to say offhandedly—because freedom does in fact appear to be limitless when we watch hang gliders make graceful loops as they float softly through the air above us. Apart from hang gliders, we also see a whole host of other airborne apparatuses that fulfill our desire to sprout wings: gliders, hang-gliders, parachutes, ultralight high-tech materials and sophisticated safety systems take pride of place because anyone with the desire to be borne aloft also wants to touch down gently. Airborne sportspersons above all need strong nerves and a love of adventure since in this type of activity adrenaline levels tend to climb too.

> Man sagt nicht umsonst „frei wie ein Vogel" – denn die Freiheit scheint tatsächlich grenzenlos zu sein, wenn wir den Gleitschirmflieger beobachten, der sanft und geschmeidig durch die Lüfte schwebt und seine Runden dreht. Neben ihm können wir am Himmel eine ganze Reihe weiterer Flugobjekte entdecken, die uns die ersehnten Flügel verleihen, wie Segelflugzeuge, Drachen oder Fallschirme. Hochentwickelte Technik, ultraleichte Materialien und ausgefeilte Sicherheitssysteme stehen hier im Vordergrund – denn jeder, der hoch fliegt, möchte doch auch wieder sanft landen. Verlangt werden von dem „Luftsportler" vor allem starke Nerven und Abenteuerlust, da der Adrenalinspiegel stets mit in die Höhe steigt.

Ce n'est pas en vain que l'on dit « libre comme un oiseau » – car c'est une liberté finie qui semble se dégager lorsque nous regardons les circonvolutions douces et souples du parapentiste qui flotte dans les airs. A ses côtés, nous découvrons dans le ciel toute une série d'autres objets volants qui nous prêtent les ailes tant désirées, tels les planeurs, les deltaplanes ou parachutes. Une technique de pointe, des matières ultra légères et des systèmes de sécurité très perfectionnés sont primordiales – car celui qui s'envole tient aussi à atterrir en douceur. Avoir les nerfs solides et le goût de l'aventure sont avant tout les qualités requises par le « sportif aérien » dont le taux d'adrénaline grimpe en même temps que lui.

> La frase hecha "libre como un pájaro" no se dice en vano, ya que la libertad parece ser absoluta cuando observamos un parapente descender suavemente en círculos desde las alturas. En el cielo se puede contemplar toda una serie de objetos volantes que nos prestan las ansiadas alas, como aeroplanos de vuelo sin motor, ala delta o paracaídas. El desarrollo de la técnica, los materiales ultraligeros y el perfeccionamiento de los sistemas de seguridad son aquí una prioridad, ya que todo aquel que quiere llegar alto, también desea aterrizar suavemente. Los deportistas del aire deben tener nervios de acero y un espíritu aventurero, puesto que el nivel de adrenalina llega hasta el límite.

Streakwing >
by Airborne

< 138

139 >

Wizard >
by Airborne

Full >
by Airborne

Lo Angar >
by Airborne

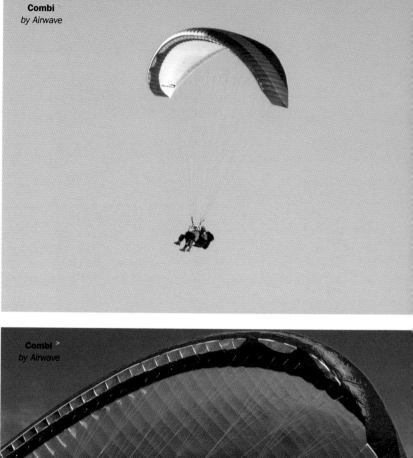

Combi
by Airwave

Combi >
by Airwave

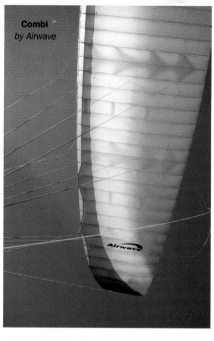

Combi >
by Airwave

< Magic
by Airwave

Magic >
by Airwave

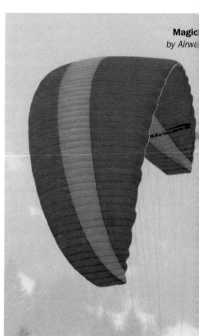

Magic
by Airwave

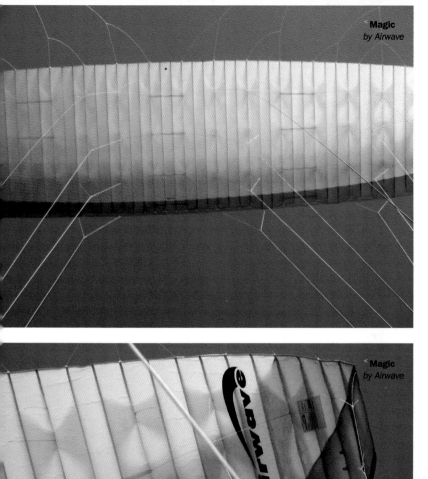

Magic
by Airwave

Magic
by Airwave

Wave
by Airwave

Force >
by Gaastra

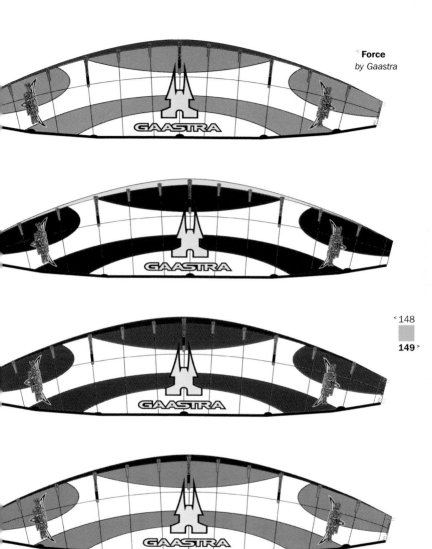

Force
by Gaastra

‹ 148

149 ›

GXR >
by Gaastra

Phoenix >
by Gaastra

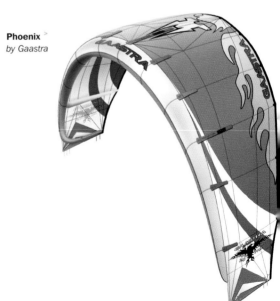

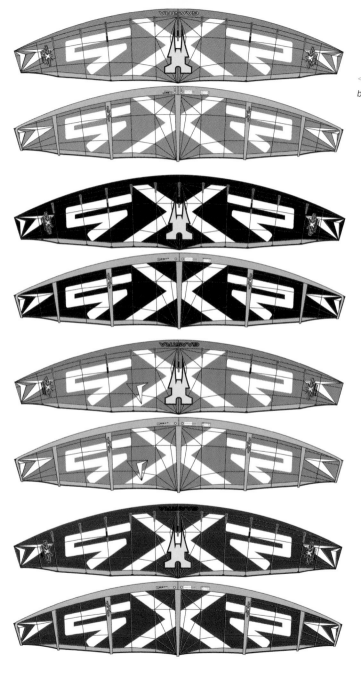

< 150
151 >

AMP
by Wipika

Core
by Wipika

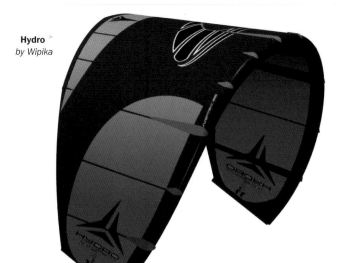

Hydro >
by Wipika

Hydro >
by Wipika

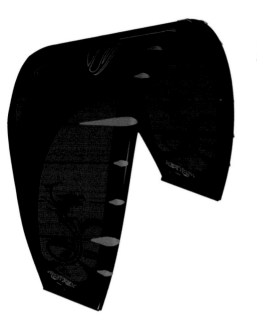

Matrix
by Wipika

Matrix
by Wipika

Boxer
by Naish

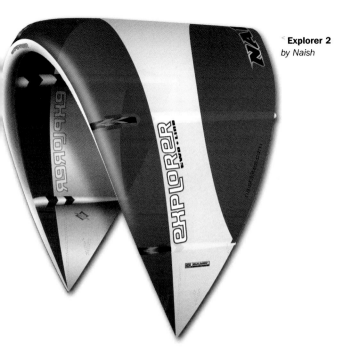

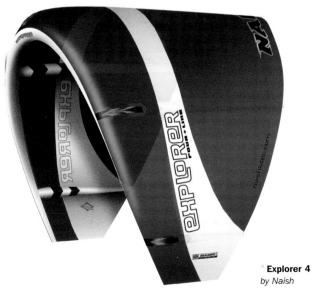

‹ **Explorer 4**
by Naish

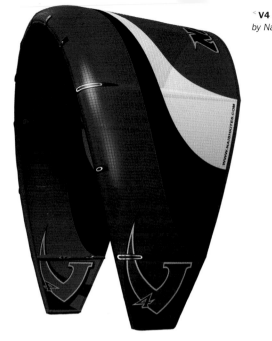

V4
by Naish

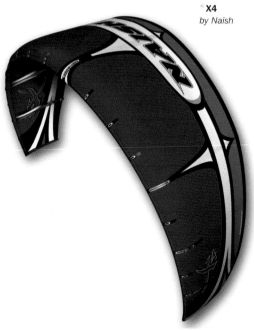

X4
by Naish

< **Xeon**
by Naish

> Narrow winding roads in mountainous landscapes, emerald green pastures ensconced in lovely valleys or lapidary coves: our love of sports takes us to a host of natural environments, whether we're mountain biking, golfing or playing volleyball on the beach. Even cities are rife with rollerbladers, basketball players and joggers giving free rein to their physical vitality. And in inclement weather, we can always resort to our local fitness club. Air cushioned shoes, ultralight fabrics, as well as clothing that absorbs perspiration bring these pleasures to near perfection. Sports product design also has an effect on fashion quite apart from the realm of athletics because, after all, dark sunglasses look stylish on lots of occasions other than bike riding.

> Kleine Sträßchen, die sich durch eine Gebirgslandschaft schlängeln, leuchtend grüne Wiesen, eingebettet in sanfte Täler, ein weiter Sandstrand – sei es mit dem Mountainbike, Golf spielend oder bei einer Partie Beach-Volleyball – sportlich erobern wir die schönsten Flecken unserer Erde. Sogar mitten in Großstädten wimmelt es von Rollerbladern, Fußballern oder Joggern, die ihrer Energie freien Lauf lassen. Bei schlechtem Wetter darf es auch gerne einmal ein Fitnessclub oder eine Sporthalle sein. Luftgepolsterte Schuhe, schweißabsorbierende Kleidung und ultraleichte Materialien machen den Genuss vollkommen. Das Design der Sportartikel hat auch Einfluss auf die Modetrends abseits sportlicher Betätigung, denn die getönte Sonnenbrille sieht nicht nur beim Radfahren gut aus.

Petites routes qui serpentent dans un paysage de montagne, prairies d'un vert éclatant nichées au creux de douces vallées, longue plage de sable fin – que ce soit en vélo tout terrain, en jouant au golf ou en faisant une partie de volley de plage – grâce au sport, nous nous emparons des plus jolis coins de la terre. Même le cœur des grandes villes fourmille de rollers, joueurs de foot ou joggers qui laissent libre cours à leur énergie. S'il fait mauvais temps, on peut aussi aller une fois au club de mise en forme ou en salle de sport. Chaussures à coussin d'air, vêtement anti-transpiration et matériel ultra léger font que le plaisir est total. Le design des articles de sport n'est pas sans avoir une influence sur les tendances de la mode en dehors du sport. En effet, les lunettes de soleil teintées sont aussi chics ailleurs que sur un vélo!

Caminos que se abren paso entre paisajes montañosos, hermosos valles que albergan prados de un verde esmeralda o amplias playas de arena: ya sea con una bicicleta todoterreno, jugando al golf o en un partido de voleibol, todos podemos conquistar deportivamente los rincones más hermosos de nuestro planeta. Incluso en el centro de las grandes ciudades hay infinidad de patinadores, futbolistas o corredores que dejan fluir toda su energía. Si el tiempo no acompaña, siempre nos queda la posibilidad de ir al gimnasio o al club deportivo. Zapatillas con cámaras de aire, sudaderas y materiales ultraligeros hacen que el placer sea completo. El diseño de los artículos de deporte influye también en la moda, tendencias que van más allá del campo deportivo, ya que las gafas con cristales de colores no sólo sientan bien a los ciclistas...

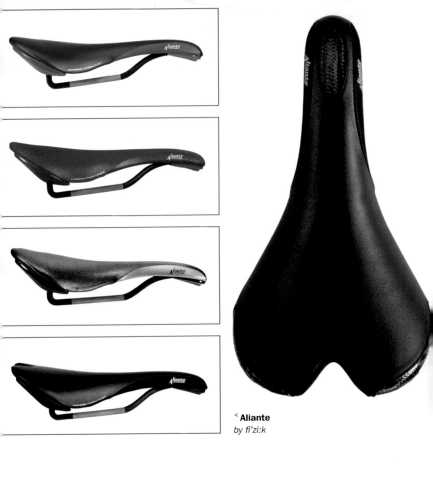

< **Aliante**
by fi'zi:k

< **Gobi**
by fi'zi:k

Petrol Evo >
by Mondraker

< 164

165

< **Arione**
by fi'zi:k

< **Foxy**
by Mondraker

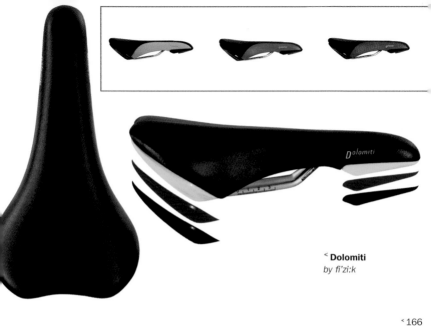

Dolomiti
by fi'zi:k

MR 81
by Mondraker

< AFX 300
by Conor

< AFX 8500
by Conor

DE 09
Conor

< 168
169 >

XRC 10
Conor

< **WRC 2 Disc**
by Conor

< **WRC 3 Disc**
by Conor

C 30
Conor

‹ 170

171 ›

C 500
Conor

< **AVALON**
by Conor

< **TULUMA 5**
by Conor

<² RAP 205
by Conor

<² XC 37
by Conor

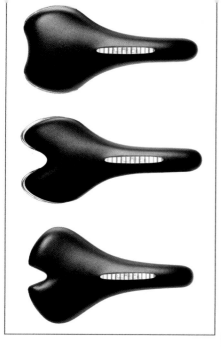

< **Pavé**
by fi'zi:k

< **Nisene**
by fi'zi:k

< **Vitesse**
by fi'zi:k

Nisene >
by fi'zi:k

Pavé >
by fi'zi:k

Vitesse >
by fi'zi:k

[<] **Curve**
by Mondraker

[<] **Cubrebotas Expe**
by Boreal

[<] 174
¹⁷⁵ [>]

[<] **G1 Expe**
by Boreal

[<] **Tierra**
by Asolo

[<] **Axis**
by Asolo

< **Attack 2.0**
by K2

< **Sir Bill**
by Coluer-Mayoral

Kato II
by Nike

Runaway
by Northwave

< **5200 Smoke Carbon**
by Trek

< **1400**
by Trek

< **Fuel 100**
by Trek

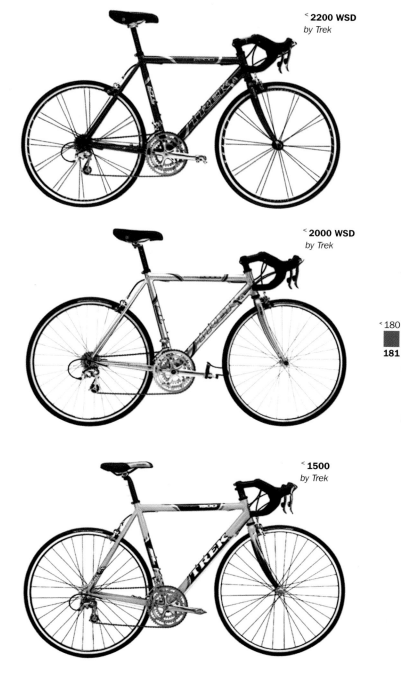

2200 WSD
by Trek

2000 WSD
by Trek

1500
by Trek

180
181

< **Orca TDF**
by Orbea

< **Orca TDE**
by Orbea

< **Comp Vitesse**
by Orbea

< 184
185 >

< **Comp Liege**
by Orbea

< **Pro Dauphin**
by Orbea

< **Pro Vento**
by Orbea

Sport Marmolada
by Orbea

< B & G Tiger
by Orbea

< B & G Bear
by Orbea

< 188
189 >

< B & G Rocker
by Orbea

[<] **P ZeroCorsa**
by Pirelli

< **Y-3**
by Adidas

< **Space II**
by Vaude

< **Mosquito**
by Vaude

< **Double root for mosquito**
by Vaude

<^ **Ferret Vaasa**
by Vaude

< 192
193 >

<^ **Ferret I**
by Vaude

<^ **Ferret I with sun-sail**
by Vaude

< **Tornado Camp**
by Vaude

< **Tornado**
by Vaude

< **Division Dome**
by Vaude

< **Opera**
by Vaude

< **Light Wing Ultralight**
by Vaude

< **Taurus Ultralight**
by Vaude

< **Odyssee**
by Vaude

< 196

197 >

Fullbody Harness
< **Complete**
by Singing Rock

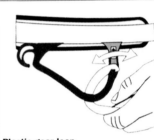

Moulded plastic gear loop

Climbing Harness

< **Blues**
by Singing Rock

Plastic gear loop

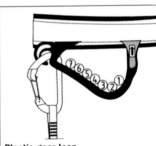

Plastic gear loop

Climbing Harness

< **Jazz**
by Singing Rock

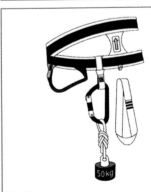

Haul loop

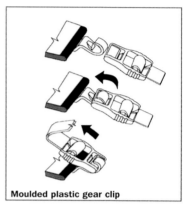

Moulded plastic gear clip

imbing Harness
Reggae
Singing Rock

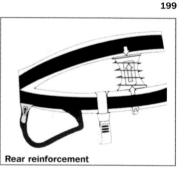

Rear reinforcement

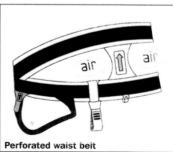

Perforated waist beit

imbing Harness
Soul
Singing Rock

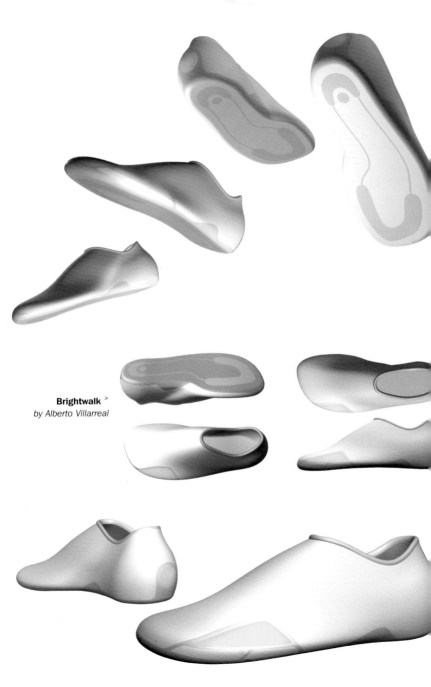

Brightwalk >
by Alberto Villarreal

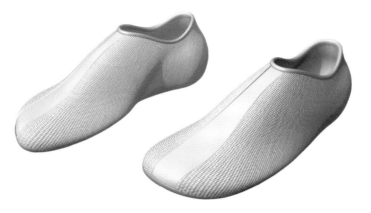

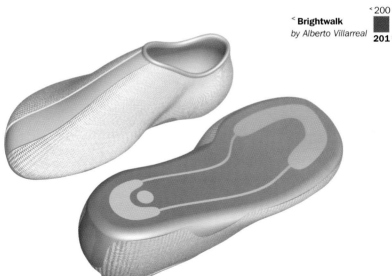

TPS Highland >
by Asolo

scalade
Asolo

[<] **Adrenaline**
by Asolo

xplorer
Asolo

[<] **Gravity**
by Asolo

[<] 202
203 [>]

PS Highland
Asolo

[<] **Mission**
by Asolo

Climbing Shoes

< **AS**
by Boreal

Balle
by Bo

< **Diablo**
by Boreal

Zephy
by Bor

ser
Boreal

Pyros >
by Boreal

nja
Boreal

Stingma >
by Boreal

< **Zen**
by Boreal

Quantu
by Bo

< **Spider**
by Boreal

Shado
by Bo

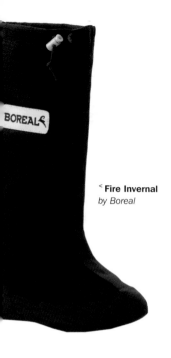

< Fire Invernal
by Boreal

< Ninja Invernal
by Boreal

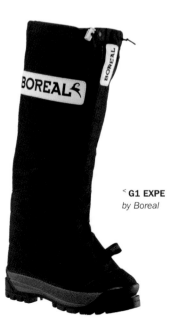

< Cubrebotas EXPE
by Boreal

< G1 EXPE
by Boreal

[<] **Bulnes**
by Boreal

[<] **Superlatok**
by Boreal

[<] **Mali**
by Boreal

[<] **Mera**
by Boreal

[<] **Pamir Lady**
by Boreal

[<] **Asan**
by Boreal

<< **Fugitive**
by Asolo

< 208

209 >

< **TPS Brenta**
by Asolo

< **Phantom**
by Asolo

< **Expe**
by Boreal

< **Ski**
by Boreal

< **Trail**
by Boreal

an
by Asolo

< **Peak**
by Asolo

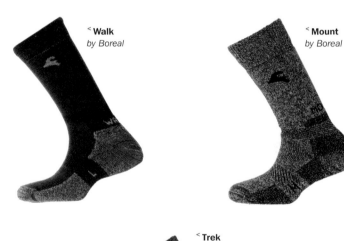

< **Walk**
by Boreal

< **Mount**
by Boreal

< 210

211 >

< **Trek**
by Boreal

< **Atlas Lady**
by Boreal

< **Namib**
by Boreal

< **Trotter**
by Boreal

< **Trisul**
by Boreal

< **Ketil**
by Boreal

< **Pisco**
by Boreal

< **Tundra**
by Boreal

< **Thor**
by Boreal

< 212
213 >

< **Tepui Lady**
by Boreal

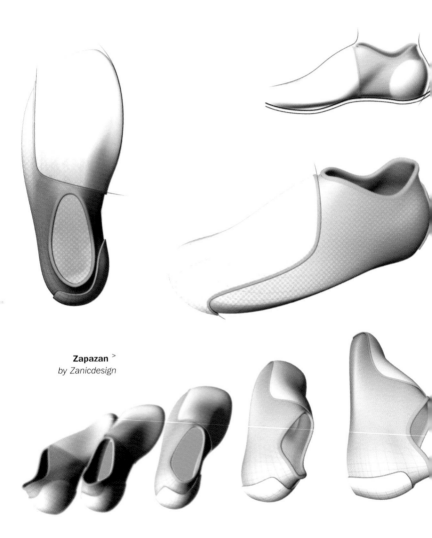

Zapazan >
by Zanicdesign

‹ 214

215 ›

Zapazan ›
by Zanicdesign

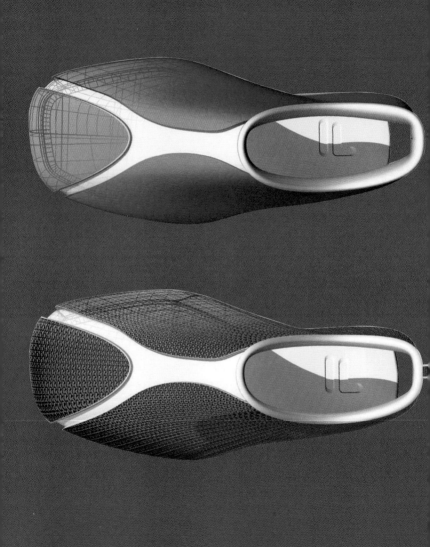

Footwear Lifestyle >
by Fila
by Alberto Villarreal

< **Tracy Macgrady**
by Adidas

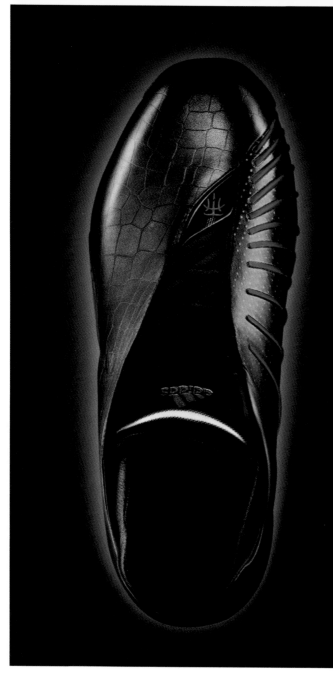

< **A3 Anthene**
by Adidas

‹ 220

221 ›

< **A3 F50**
by Adidas

< 222
223 >

^{<} **A3 Ultraride**
by Adidas

< 224

225 >

A3 Ultraride
by Adidas

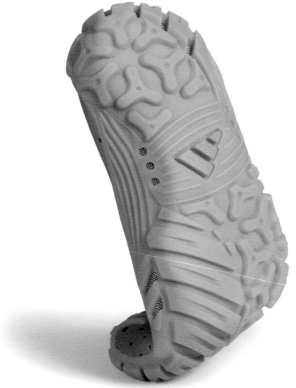

< Carnuba
by Adidas

‹ 228
229 ›

3 Superstar Ultra
Adidas

< **Clima Cool**
by Adidas

< 230
231 >

< **Clima Cool**
by Adidas

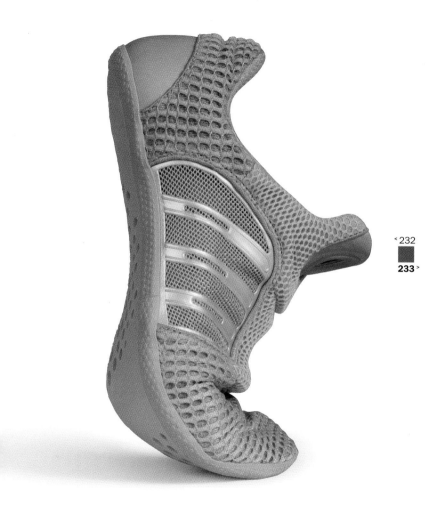

< 232

233 >

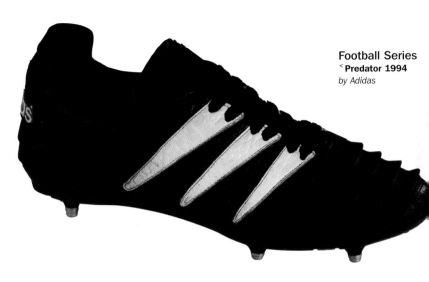

Football Series
< **Predator 1994**
by Adidas

Predator II 1995 >
by Adidas

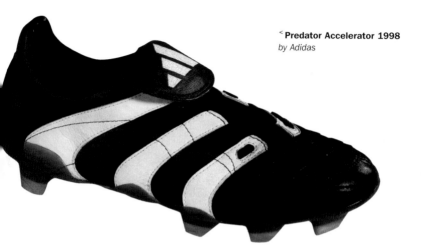

Predator Accelerator 1998
by Adidas

< 234
235 >

Predator Precision 2000
by Adidas

[<] **Pedinare**
by Reebok

[<] **TC Rampante II MS**
by Reebok

1618 [>]
by Reebok

IKER
CASILLAS

^{<} **Foster Millenium Sprint**
by Reebok

^{<} **Game Day TMX**
by Reebok

nterro
Reebok

^{<} **Valental**
by Reebok

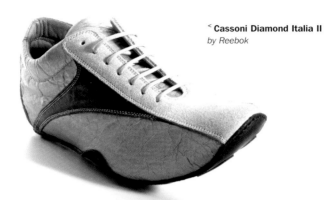

Cassoni Diamond Italia II
by Reebok

Cassoni Diamond Italia DLX
by Reebok

< Victory Handbag
by Reebok

< 238
239 >

< AM Sports Bag
by Reebok

< Survivor Ball Backpack
by Reebok

Air Zoom Total 90 III >
by Nike

< 240

241 >

< **Air Zoom Total 90 III**
by Nike

Mercurial Vapor Black
by Nike

Mercurial Vapor Blue
by Nike

Mercurial Vapor Red
by Nike

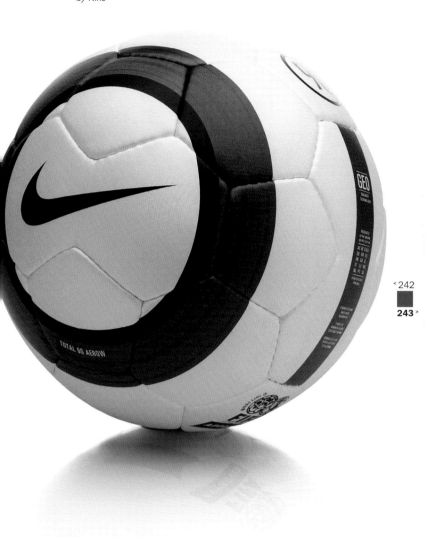

< **Total 90 Aerow**
by Nike

[<]**Total 90 Aerow**
by Nike

Total 90 Aerow [>]
by Nike

Total 90 Wired [>]
by Nike

Zoom Total 90 >
by Nike

< 246
247 >

< **Roteiro**
by Adidas

Driver
ERC Fusion >
by Calaway

 ERC Fusion
by Calaway

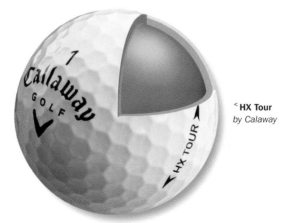

 HX Tour
by Calaway

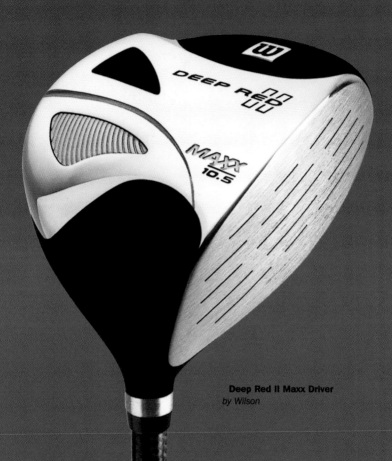

Deep Red II Maxx Driver
by Wilson

^{< 252}

253 >

eep Red II Distance
Wilson

[<] **Deep Red II Distance Fairway Woods**
by Wilson

ilson Staff Golf Balls
Wilson

< **Deep Red II Tour Irons**
by Wilson

< **Dyna-Powered Gun-Metal Wedges**
by Wilson

Wilson Staff True Tour Elite
by Wilson

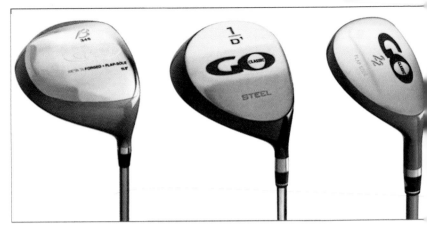

Golf Clubs

^{<} **Go Classic Beta 345 Driver**
by Go Classic

^{<} **Go Classic Woods**
by Go Classic

^{<} **Go Classic Wizard**
by Go Classic

^{<} **Go Classic Irons**
by Go Classic

^{<} **Go Classic Matrix**
by Go Classic

^{<} **Go Classic LPW Irons**
by Go Classic

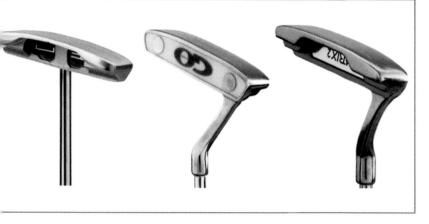

o Classic in Putter
Go Classic

<**Go Classic Matrix Putters**
  (left hand)
  by Go Classic

<**Go Classic Matrix Putters**
  (right hand)
  by Go Classic

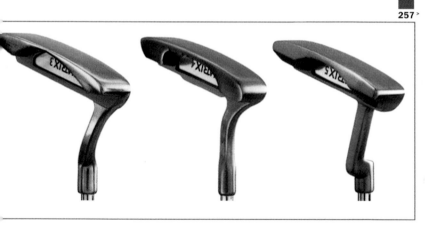

o Classic Matrix Putters
ight hand)
Go Classic

<**Go Classic Matrix Putters**
  (right hand)
  by Go Classic

<**Go Classic Matrix Putters**
  (right hand)
  by Go Classic

< **Deep Red II Distance Irons**
by Wilson

< **Deep Red II Iron Shafts**
by Wilson

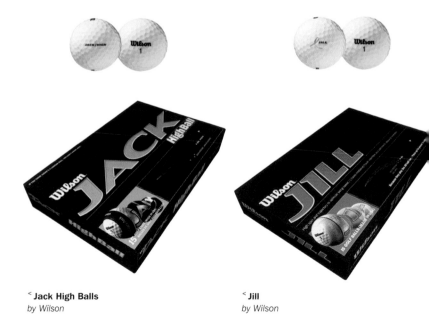

< **Jack High Balls**
by Wilson

< **Jill**
by Wilson

< **Jack Long Balls**
by Wilson

< **Jack Spin Balls**
by Wilson

Golf Gloves

< **Pro fit**
by Wilson

< **Dual+fit**
by Wilson

Vision Series. Tennis Shoes
[<] **Crossfire SL**
by Wilson

Vision Series. Tennis Shoes
[<] **Crossfire**
by Wilson

Vision Series. Tennis Shoes

< **Fli-By**
by Wilson

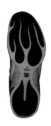

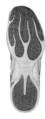

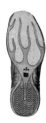

Vision Series. Tennis Shoes
< **Fantom**
by Wilson

< **T2 New TRIAD 2 118"**
by Wilson

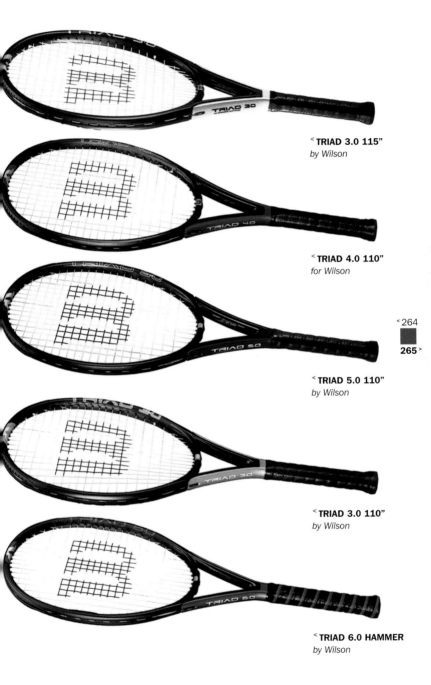

[<] **TRIAD 3.0 115"**
by Wilson

[<] **TRIAD 4.0 110"**
for Wilson

[<] 264

265 [>]

[<] **TRIAD 5.0 110"**
by Wilson

[<] **TRIAD 3.0 110"**
by Wilson

[<] **TRIAD 6.0 HAMMER**
by Wilson

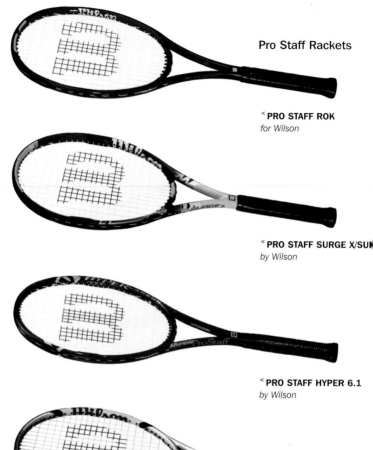

Pro Staff Rackets

< **PRO STAFF ROK**
for Wilson

< **PRO STAFF SURGE X/SU**
by Wilson

< **PRO STAFF HYPER 6.1**
by Wilson

< **PRO STAFF ZONE**
by Wilson

< **PRO STAFF TORCH**
by Wilson

mium Performance Strings

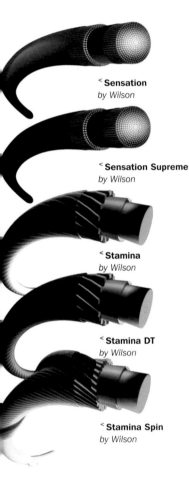

[<] **Sensation**
by Wilson

[<] **Sensation Supreme**
by Wilson

[<] **Stamina**
by Wilson

[<] **Stamina DT**
by Wilson

[<] **Stamina Spin**
by Wilson

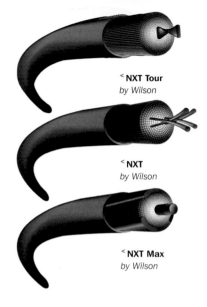

[<] **NXT Tour**
by Wilson

[<] **NXT**
by Wilson

[<] **NXT Max**
by Wilson

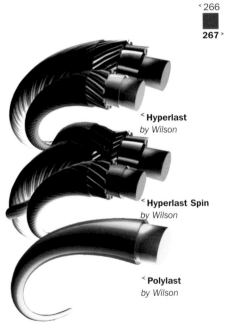

[<] **Hyperlast**
by Wilson

[<] **Hyperlast Spin**
by Wilson

[<] **Polylast**
by Wilson

< **A3000X1 KIP LEATHER (Infielder)**
by Wilson

< **A2000 1915 PRO-STOCK LEATHER (Pitcher)**
by Wilson

< **A1000 VORTEX LEATHER (Outfielder)**
by Wilson

DEMARIN ADULT BASEBALL BATS
Wilson

DEMARIN ADULT BASEBALL BATS
Wilson

Baseballs

< **A1001BSST For Collegiate and High School Play**
by Wilson

< **A1010BPROSST For Collegiate and High School Play**
by Wilson

< **A1010BHS1SST For Collegiate and
High School Play**
by Wilson

< **A1028BYEL For High School and Adult
Indoor Pratice, Youth League Play**
by Wilson

**A1030B For High School and Adult Practice,
Youth League Play**
by Wilson

**A1030BYEL For High School and Adult
Indoor/Outdoor Practice, Youth League Play**
by Wilson

< 270

271 >

**A1228B For Minor League and
Coach Pitch Play**
by Wilson

< **A1217B For Coach Pitch and
T-Ball Play**
by Wilson

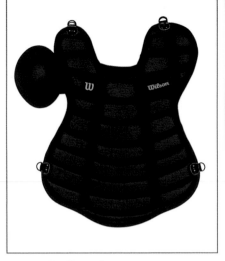

Baseballs Chest Protectors

< **18" Professional Thermo-foam Chest Protector**
by Wilson

< **18¹/₂" Pro Orlon Chest Protector**
by Wilson

< **18¹/₂" Ensolite® Chest Protector**
by Wilson

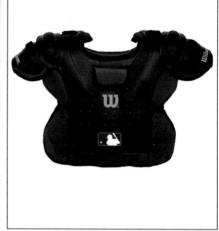

3210 Wilson Professional Gold est Protector
Wilson

< **A3215 Wilson Professional Platinum Chest Protector**
by Wilson

< **A3209 Wilson Professional Chest Protector**
by Wilson

Footballs Series

< **Precision E.X.G**
by Uhlsport

< **Goalkeeper MD**
by Uhlsport

< **Velocity SC**
by Uhlsport

< **Absolutgrip Ergonomic Supportframe**
by Uhlsport

< **360° Touch Supersoft**
by Uhlsport

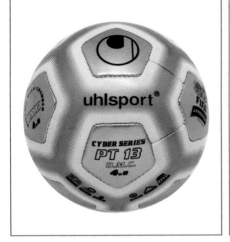

Footballs Cyber Series

< **Cyber Series PT 13 D.M.C 4.0**
by Uhlsport

< **Cyber Series PT 13 Professional D.M.S**
by Uhlsport

< **Cyber Series PT 13 Professional D.C.S**
by Uhlsport

Cyber Series 290 Ultra Lite
by Uhlsport

< **Cyber Series MYTHOS**
by Uhlsport

< **Cyber Series PRISMA**
by Uhlsport

Motor Sport Jacket
by Puma

7CH Hoodie
by Puma

Ringer Logo Tee
by Puma

Kas SL Tee
by Puma

Land Polo
by Puma

Cat Cargo Pant
by Puma

Ringer Tee
Puma

<Track Jacket**
by Puma

<278

279 >

<Skirt**
by Puma

<Para Skirt**
by Puma

< **Ranger Balk Tank**
by Puma

< **Nº 1 Logo Hoodie**
by Puma

< **Track Jacket**
by Puma

< **Dress**
by Puma

< **Bootleg Jazz Pant**
by Puma

[<] **Sprint Shoulder Bag**
by Puma

[<] **Bigcat Back Palk**
by Puma

[<] **Tennis Bag**
by Puma

[<]280

281[>]

[<] **Cat Cotton Belt**
by Puma

[<] **New Edition Shopper**
by Puma

< **Bluto Stich**
by Puma

< **Ez Slider**
by Puma

< **Sprint Clog Women's**
by Puma

< **Mostro Leather**
by Puma

< 282

283 >

< **Brush Spike**
by Puma

< **Mostro Leather Women's**
by Puma

<^ **Criatura Leather**
by Puma

<^ **Calibro I**
by Puma

<^ **Mostro Garment**
by Puma

< **Complete's Spike**
by Puma

< **Hiro**
by Puma

< **Red Planet**
by Puma

< **Asana Women's**
by Puma

< **Rennbahn'!**
by Puma

< **Mostro Perf.**
by Puma

< **Schatten Boxen Suede**
by Puma

< **Schatten Boxen**
by Puma

< **Mono Alto Women's**
by Puma

< **Rennkatze II Hi**
by Puma

< **Rennkatze**
by Puma

< **Toure**
by Puma

‹ 288
289 ›

‹ **MY-9 Low**
by Puma

<MY-9 Low
by Puma

290 >
291 >

< **MY-9 Mid**
by Puma

< **MY-10 M**
by Puma

< 292
293 >

< **Fioretto Alto**
by Puma

Cerchion
by Puma

< 294

295 >

< **Macchina**
by Puma

<Artikel 610
by Puma

< 296
297 >

< **Artikel 76**
by Puma

<Artikel 610
by Puma

‹ 298
299 ›

‹ **van Slobbe Rennschuh Brogue**
by Puma

van Slobbe Rennschuh
by Puma

< **van Slobbe Sprint Logo Wn's**
by Puma

< Swift Dri-FIT Half Zip Te
by Nike

< Swift Dri-FIT Short Sleeve To
by Nike

<Swift Clima-FIT Convertible Jacket**
by Nike

< 302

303 >

< Swift Dri-FIT Capri Tight
by Nike

< Swift
by Nike

< 304
305 >

< **Dunk**
by Nike

< 310

311 >

< **Vapor Control**
by Nike

Master Mid
by Nike

312
313

Talaria
by Nike

Zoom City Vapor
by Nike

<314

315>

Kokoro
by Nike

< Greco Low
by Nike

< Air Max Desire
by Nike

Janeiro Sandal
by Nike

< **Sandals**
by Nike

< **Sandals**
by Nike

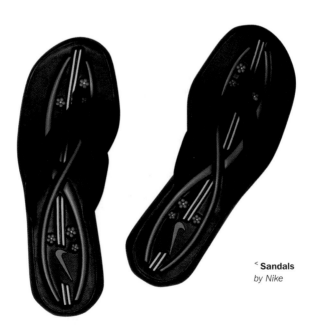

< **Sandals**
by Nike

< **Womens Imara**
by Nike

< **Sun Sport Tote**
by Nike

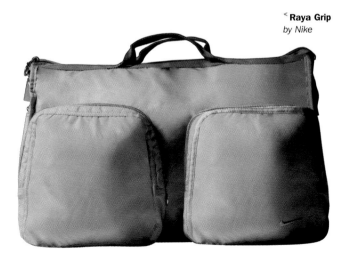

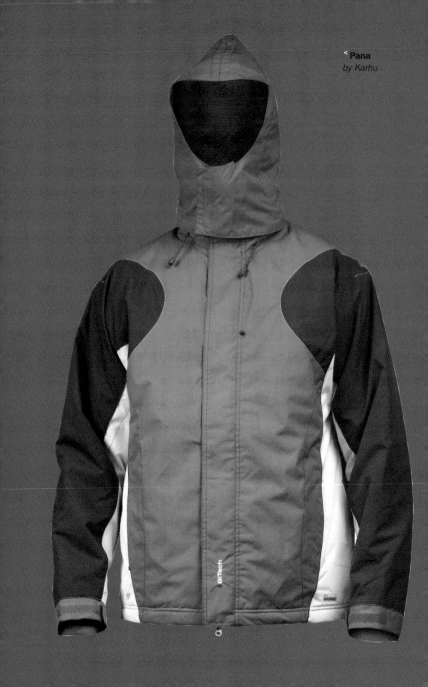

Pirita
by Karhu

322 >
323 >

Paulus >
by Karhu

< Pekka
by Karhu

Pisto ^>
by Karhu

< Pellervo
by Karhu

Rimas
by Karhu

324 >
325 >

Recent >
by Karhu

< Surf Lifestyle
by Quiksilver

Multisport >
by Quiksilver

< 328
329 >

Ventair [>]
by Kangol

Fresh Mesh [>]
by Kangol

[<] 330

331 [>]

ntair Spacecap [>]
by Kangol

**Tropic Ventair
Snipe** >
by Kangol

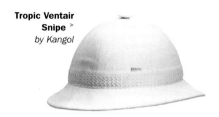

Tropic Bin >
by Kangol

Tropic Lahinch >
by Kangol

Tropic Diva >
by Kangol

Tropic Casual >
by Kangol

Tropic Trilby >
by Kangol

opic Monty >
by Kangol

Tropic Enfield >
by Kangol

**ropic Stretch
Skull Cap** >
by Kangol

**Two Tone
Reversible Bell** >
by Kangol

< 332

333 >

**pic Chequers
Spacecap** >
by Kangol

**Tropic Chequers
Bell** >
by Kangol

**Tropic Ripple
Stripe Bin** >
by Kangol

**Tropic Ripple
Stripe Spacecap** >
by Kangol

**Tropic Ripple
Stripe** >
by Kangol

**Tropic Kangol
Jacquard
4 Panel Bell** >
by Kangol

**Tropic Kangol
Jacquard Bin** >
by Kangol

Bermuda Casual >
by Kangol

Bermuda Lahinch >
by Kangol

muda Diva >
by Kangol

Cotton Crusher >
by Kangol

< 334

335 >

ton Reefer >
by Kangol

Tropic Wendy >
by Kangol

Cotton Beret >
by Kangol

**Fully Fashioned
Cotton Skull Cap** >
by Kangol

**Towelling
Kamarood
Reversible
Lahinch** >
by Kangol

Denim Bin >
by Kangol

**Atomic Intarsia
Cloche** >
by Kangol

**Atomic
Jacquard Bell** >
by Kangol

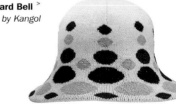

**Crochet
Fabric Diva** >
by Kangol

**Crochet Paper/Fabric
Lahinch** >
by Kangol

**Check/Teflon
Reversible
Lahinch** >
by Kangol

< 336

337 >

**Crochet Rib
Spitfire** >
by Kangol

**Cotton Drill
Visor** >
by Kangol

> Already in our mother's wombs, we are immersed in water, and so it's little wonder that human beings feel a particularly strong connection to and so enjoy this medium, through which we move nearly weightlessly. California surfers give us a glimpse of paradise when they gambol on the crest of a huge wave with their surfboard, let themselves be carried along by it and then, just as the wave breaks, plunge beneath it. But even the non-surfers among us can experience harmonious oneness with water through swimming, sailing, windsurfing, water-skiing or scuba diving. State of the art body suits and highly responsive materials are indispensable equipment for untrammeled enjoyment of water sports.

> Schon im Mutterleib ist der Embryo rund um von Wasser umgeben, und so ist es nicht verwunderlich, dass der Mensch zu diesem Element eine ganz besondere Verbundenheit verspürt und es genießt, sich nahezu schwerelos darin fortzubewegen. Der kalifornische Wellenreiter macht es uns vor, wenn er mit seinem Surfboard auf dem Kamm einer gigantischen Welle tanzt, sich von ihr davontragen lässt und schließlich genau an dem Punkt, wo sie sich bricht, unter ihr wegtaucht. Schwimmend oder auch beim Segeln, Windsurfen, Wasserskifahren oder Tauchen können wir den harmonischen Einklang mit dem Wasser finden. Um den Wassersport ungetrübt genießen zu können, sind modernste Thermoanzüge und hochdynamische Materialien unverzichtbar.

Déjà dans le ventre de la mère, l'embryon est entouré d'eau. Ce n'est donc pas étonnant que l'homme se sente particulièrement lié à cet élément et adore y évoluer presque en état d'apesanteur. C'est ce que nous montre le surfeur californien, lorsqu'il danse avec sa planche de surf sur la crête d'une vague gigantesque, se laisse porter par elle et juste à l'endroit où elle se brise, plonge en dessous. La natation ou la voile, la planche à voile, le ski nautique ou la plongée nous permettent d'être en harmonie avec l'eau. Profiter des sports aquatiques sans encombre, ne va pas sans les indispensables combinaisons isolantes les plus modernes et un matériel de pointe très rapide.

Ya en el vientre de la madre estamos rodeados de agua, así que no es de extrañar que el ser humano tenga una especial predilección por ese medio y disfrute de la posibilidad que le brinda de moverse con cierta sensación de ingravidez. Los surfistas californianos nos ofrecen el espectáculo de bailar sobre olas gigantes, dejarse llevar por ellas y, justo en el lugar donde rompen, desaparecer bajo las aguas. Y es que con la práctica de deportes como la natación, la vela, el windsurf, el esquí acuático o el submarinismo podemos sentirnos en perfecta armonía con el líquido elemento. Pero para poder disfrutar al máximo de estos deportes acuáticos no podemos prescindir de las más modernas innovaciones, como trajes térmicos y materiales hidrodinámicos.

Windsurf Sails
RS4 ˃
Slalom and Formula
by Neilpryde

< 342
343 >

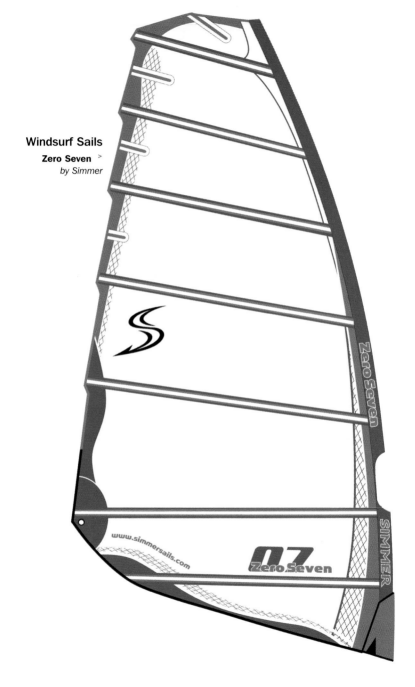

Windsurf Sails

Zero Seven >
by Simmer

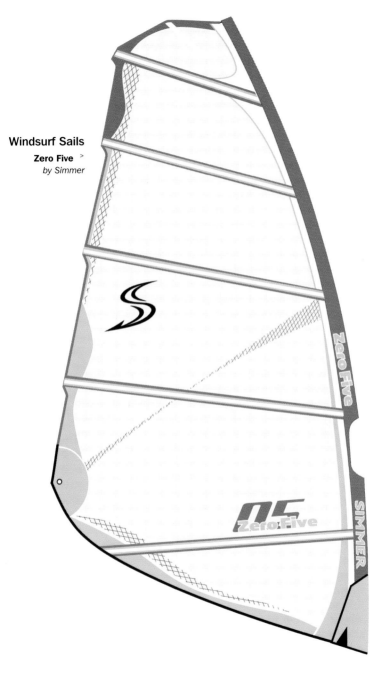

Windsurf Sails

Zero Five >
by Simmer

< 344

345 >

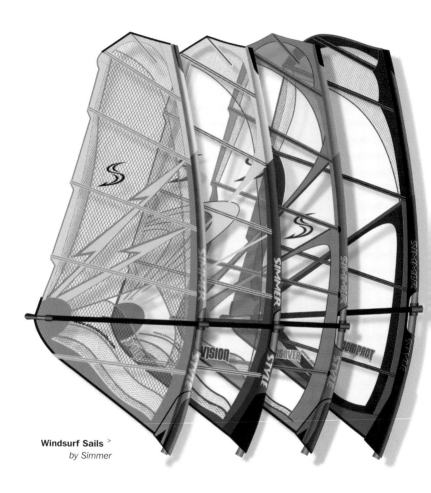

Windsurf Sails >
by Simmer

Smoothie >
by Simmer

< 346
347 >

Windsurf Sails

Freerace >
by Simmer

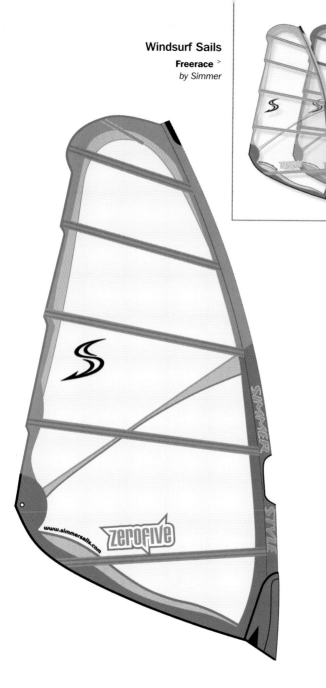

Windsurf Sails

Zero Seven. Freerace no cambers [>]
by Simmer

[<] 348

349 [>]

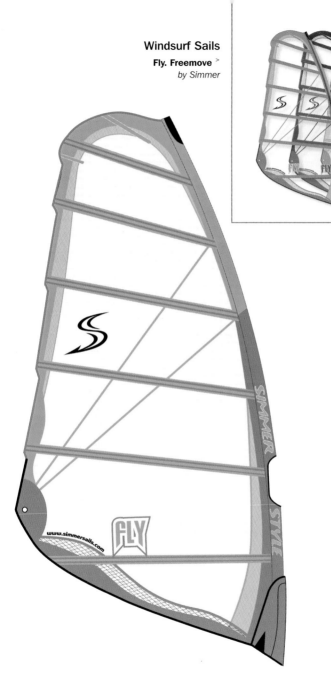

Windsurf Sails

Fly. Freemove >
by Simmer

< 350

351 >

< **Kitty (KIT04)**
by Cobian

< **Koi (KOI04)**
by Cobian

< **Flores (FRS04)**
by Cobian

< **Rosa (ROS04**
by Cobian

[<] **Sponger (SP004)**
by Cobian

[<] **Latigo (LAT04)**
by Cobian

[<] 352

353 [>]

[<] **Nomad (NOM04)**
by Cobian

[<] **Dakota (DAK04)**
by Cobian

< **Airlab**
by Mares

< **Morphos Twin**
by Mares

< **Plana Avanti Qua**
by Mares

< **Plana Avanti X3**
by Mares

< **Plana Avanti Tre**
by Mares

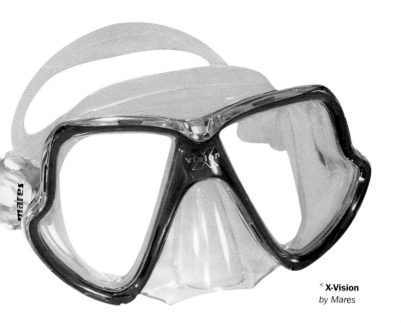

< **X-Vision**
by Mares

< 356

357 >

< **Esa**
by Mares

< **X-Vision**
by Mares

< **Mariner**
by Mares

< **Kiev**
by Turbo

< **Prague**
by Turbo

< 358

359 >

< **Los Angeles**
by Turbo

< **Los Angeles JR.**
by Turbo

< **Berlin**
by Turbo

< **Stockhol**
by Turbo

< **Osaka**
by Turbo

< **Athens**
by Turbo

< **Mexico**
by Turbo

< **London**
by Turbo

^{<} **Lycra band**
by Turbo

^{<} **Lycra**
by Turbo

^{<} **Male lycra**
by Turbo

^{<} 360

361 ^{>}

^{<} **Silicone Gold/Silver/Bronze**
by Turbo

^{<} **Silicone Vol. Multiturbo**
by Turbo

^{<} **Silicone Shark**
by Turbo

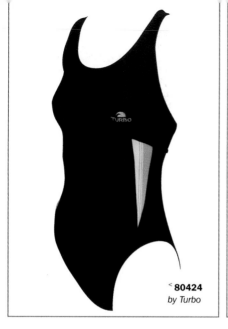

< **80424**
by Turbo

< **80425**
by Turbo

< **80426**
by Turbo

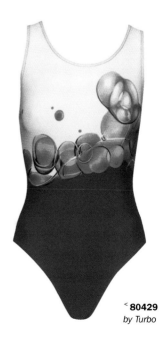

< **80429**
by Turbo

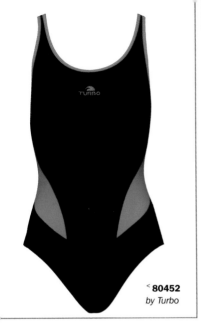

< **80452**
by Turbo

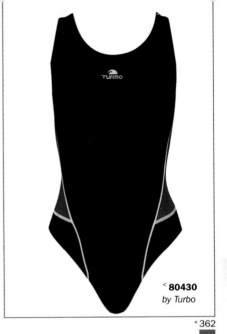

< **80430**
by Turbo

<362
363 >

< **80433**
by Turbo

< **80435**
by Turbo

< **80452**
by Turbo

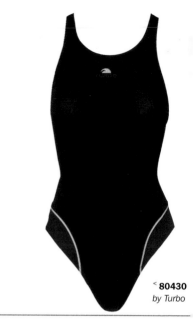

< **80430**
by Turbo

< **80433**
by Turbo

< **80435**
by Turbo

Waterpolo Series

< **Stars**
by Turbo

< **H20 Zoom**
by Turbo

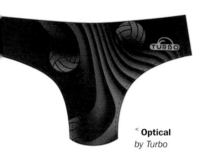

< 364

365 >

< **Optical**
by Turbo

< **Bubbles-Balls**
by Turbo

< **Jeans**
by Turbo

< **Commando**
by Turbo

< **Devil**
by Turbo

< **Multiskull**
by Turbo

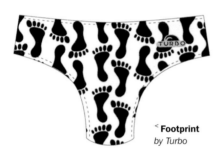

< **Footprint**
by Turbo

< **Tiger**
by Turbo

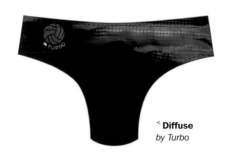

< **Diffuse**
by Turbo

< **Fish**
by Turbo

Waterpolo Series

< **Fantasy**
by Turbo

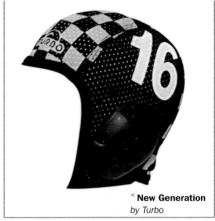

< **New Generation**
by Turbo

< 366

367 >

< **Professional**
by Turbo

< **Training**
by Turbo

Waterpolo Clothes

< **WP Polo**
by Turbo

Waterpolo Clothes

< **WP Player**
by Turbo

Waterpolo Clothes

< **WP Fire Ball**
by Turbo

Waterpolo Clothes

< **WP n5**
by Turbo

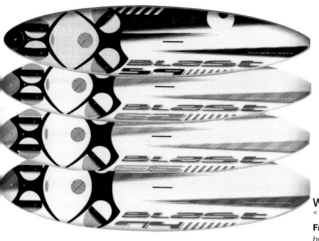

Windsurf Boards
< **Blast 59, 62, 66 & 74,
Freeride Slalom**
by Bic Sport

< 368

369 >

< **Techno II 66 & 75/66 & 75 Pro.
Freeride Race**
by Bic Sport

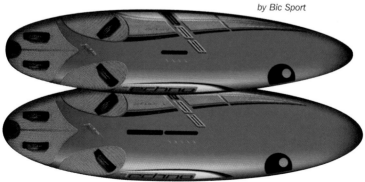

< **Techno 283 & 293d. Freeride**
by Bic Sport

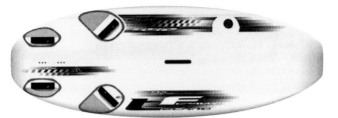

< **Techno Formula.**
Formula Windsurfing
by Bic Sport

< **FW 1.5 Daytona.**
Formula Windsurfing
by Bic Sport

< **Nova & Kid Nova. Beg**
by Bic Sport

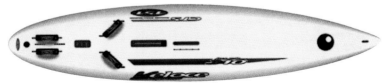

< **Veloce 310. Freeride**
by Bic Sport

<Melody. Beginners
by Bic Sport

<Power Glide 130, 145,
160 & PG CSE. Freeride
by F2

<Discovery One 30, 70, 90, 70
Sport & 90 Sport. Freeride
by F2

< **CompStyle 244 & 246**
Freestyle
by F2

< **Eliminator 240 & 242**
Supercross
by F2

< **SX 110 & 140. Slalon**
by F2

< **FX 100-II. Formula**
by F2

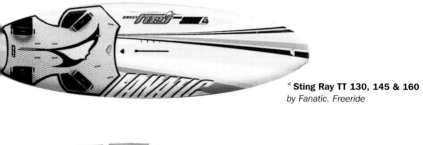

[<] **Sting Ray TT 130, 145 & 160**
by Fanatic. Freeride

[<] **Viper L & XL.
Freeride Family**
by Fanatic

[<] **Falcon Slalom & T2
Formula. Race**
by Fanatic

< **Wave 64, 69, 74, 84, & 8**
by JP Australia

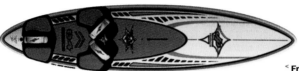

< **Freestyle Wave 77-II, 84-**
91-II & 98-II
by JP Australia

< **Freestyle 101 & 111 FWS**
101 & 111 Pro
by JP Australia

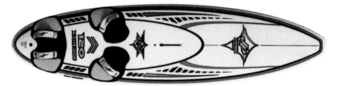

< **X- Cite 105, 120, 135 &**
150 FWS / ES
by JP Australia

< **Super-X 82, 93, 104 & 1**
FWS / ES
by JP Australia

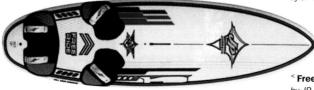

< **Freeride 128, 143 & 158**
by JP Australia

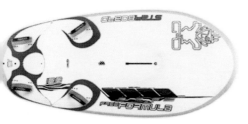

< **Carve 90, 99, 111, 121, 131, 145 & 161. Freeride**
by Starboard

< **FreeFormula 138 & 158. Freerace**
by Starboard

< 374

375 >

< **Formula 138, 158, Junior & Youth. Race**
by Starboard

< **Hypersonic 96, 111 & 133. Race**
by Starboard

< **Sonic 90, 100 & 110. High Wind Race**
by Starboard

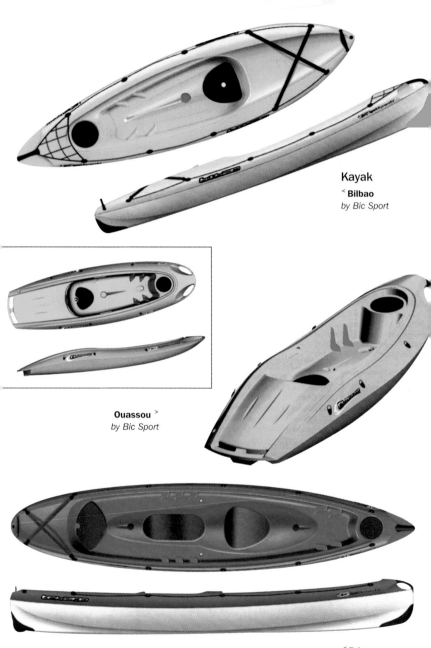

Kayak

< **Bilbao**
by Bic Sport

Ouassou >
by Bic Sport

< **Tobago**
by Bic Sport

^{<}**Yak Board**
by Ocean Kayak

^{<}**Cabo**
by Ocean Kayak

^{<}**Frenzy**
by Ocean Kayak

^{<}376

377 ^{>}

^{<}**Venus**
by Ocean Kayak

^{<}**Caper**
by Ocean Kayak

^{<}**Malibu II**
by Ocean Kayak

^{<}**Mars**
by Ocean Kayak

< Scrambler
by Ocean Kayak

< Aegean
by Ocean Kayak

< Scupper Pro TW
by Ocean Kayak

< Kea
by Ocean Kayak

< Drifter
by Ocean Kayak

< Malibu II XL
by Ocean Kayak

< **Plancha de remo inflable**
by Sevylor

< **Eskimo**
by Sevylor

< **Kayak Aguas Bravas**
by Ocean Kayak

< **Ocean Kayak**
by Sevylor

< **Kayak Polivalente**
by Sevylor

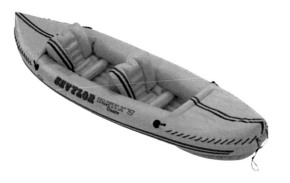

< **Tahiti**
by Ocean Kayak

< **Contact 141**
by Gaastra

< **Contact 148**
by Gaastra

< Micro
by Gaastra

< Sky
by Gaa

< Cazor
by SOS

< Cazo
by SOS

382

383

<Thorn
by Nash

< 384

385 >

< **Haze TT**
by Nash

< MTX
by Nash

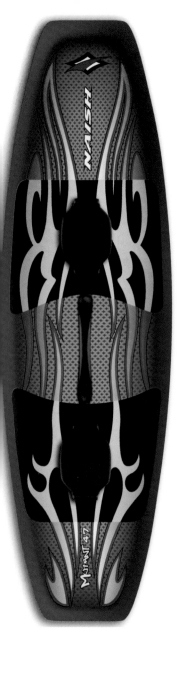

< 386
387 >

< **Mutant**
by Nash

< **Stubbie**
by Nash

<388

389>

<**TTPro 134**
by Nash

Directory >

Verzeichnis >

Répertoire >

Directorio >

[<]Snow [<]Schnee [<]Neige [<]Nieve

[<] **K2 (Marc Space)**
www.k2sport.com

[<] **Marker**
www.markerusa.com

[<] **Tecnica**
www.tecnicausa.com

[<] **Red**
www.burton.com

[<] **Völkl**
www.volkl.com

[<] **Forum**
www.forumsnowboards.

[<] **Burton**
www.burton.com

[<] **Porsche**
www.porsche.com

CliC Goggles
www.clicgoggles.com

Rossignol
www.rossignol.com

Suunto Wristop Computers
www.suunto.com

Hammer
www.hammersnowboards.com

Vaude
www.vaude.de

Bogner
www.bogner.com

Fritschi
www.fritschi.ch

Quiksilver
www.quiksilver.com

Snow <Schnee <Neige <Nieve

<**Roxy**
www.roxy.com

<**Wipika**
www.wipikakiteboarding

Air <Luft <Air <Aire

<**Airborne**
www.airborne.com.au

<**Naish**
www.naishkites.com

Earth <Erde <Terre <Tierra

<**Airwave**
www.airwave-gliders.com

<**fi'zi:k**
www.fizik.it

<**Gaastra**
www.gaastrakites.com

<**Mondraker**
www.mondraker.com

Conor
www.conor.es

Coluer by Mayoral
www.coluer.com

Boreal
www.e-boreal.com

Nike
www.nike.com

Asolo
www.asolo.com

Northwave
www.northwave.com

K2 (Marc Space)
www.k2sport.com

Trek
www.trekbikes.com

<Earth <Erde <Terre <Tierra

< **Orbea**
www.orbea.com

< **Singing Rock**
www.singingrock.com

< **Pirelli**
www.pirelli.com

< **Alberto Villarreal**
www.zanicdesign.com

< **Adidas**
www.adidas.com

< **Reebok**
www.reebok.com

< **Vaude**
www.vaude.de

< **Fila**
www.fila.com

< **Puma**
www.puma.com

< **Uhlsport**
www.uhlsport.com

< **Callaway**
www.callawaygolf.com

< **Karhu**
www.karhu.com

< **Wilson**
www.wilson.com

< **Quiksilver**
www.quiksilver.com

< **Go Classic**
www.goclassicgolf.com

< **Roxy**
www.roxy.com

Earth ⟨Erde ⟨Terre ⟨Tierra

⟨ **kangol**
www.kangol.com

⟨ **Mares**
www.mares.com

Water ⟨Wasser ⟨Eau ⟨Agua

⟨ **Neilpryde**
www.neilpryde.com

⟨ **Turbo**
www.turbo.es

⟨ **Simmer**
www.simmersails.com

⟨ **Bic Sport**
www.bicsport.com

⟨ **Cobian**
www.cobianusa.com

⟨ **F2**
www.f2.com

Fanatic (Freeride)
www.fanatic.com

Sevylor
www.sevylor.com

JP Australia
www.jp-australia.com

Gaastra
www.gaastrakites.com

Starboard
www.star-board.com

Naish
www.naishkites.com

Ocean Kayak
www.oceankayak.com

Other Designpocket titles by teNeues

African Interior Design 3-8238-4563-2
Asian Interior Design 3-8238-4527-6
Avant-Garde Page Design 3-8238-4554-3
Bathroom Design 3-8238-4523-3
Beach Hotels 3-8238-4566-7
Berlin Apartments 3-8238-5596-4
Cafés & Restaurants 3-8238-5478-X
Car Design 3-8238-4561-6
Cool Hotels 3-8238-5556-5
Cool Hotels America 3-8238-4565-9
Cosmopolitan Hotels 3-8238-4546-2
Country Hotels 3-8238-5574-3
Exhibition Design 3-8238-5548-4
Furniture Design 3-8238-5575-1
Garden Design 3-8238-4524-1
Italian Interior Design 3-8238-5495-X
Kitchen Design 3-8238-4522-5
London Apartments 3-8238-5558-1
Los Angeles Houses 3-8238-5594-8
Miami Houses 3-8238-4545-4
New York Apartments 3-8238-5557-3
Office Design 3-8238-5578-6
Paris Apartments 3-8238-5571-9
Pool Design 3-8238-4531-4
Product Design 3-8238-5597-2
Rome Houses 3-8238-4564-0
San Francisco Houses 3-8238-4526-8
Showrooms 3-8238-5496-8
Ski Hotels 3-8238-4543-8
Spa & Wellness Hotels 3-8238-5595-6
Staircases 3-8238-5572-7
Sydney Houses 3-8238-4525-X
Tokyo Houses 3-8238-5573-5
Tropical Houses 3-8238-4544-6

Each volume:

12.5 x 18.5 cm
400 pages
c. 400 color illustrations

M 411354